SHIFT

CREATING BETTER TOMORROWS:
WINNING AT WORK
AND IN LIFE

MICHAEL O'BRIEN

SHIFT

ISBN (Hardback edition): 978-0-9987328-0-0
ISBN (Paperback edition): 978-0-9987328-1-7
ISBN (eBook edition): 978-0-9987328-2-4

To learn more about Michael, please visit www.michaelob.net
and www.pelotoncc.net

Originally produced for Peloton Coaching and Consulting by:
Red Hill Publishing, LLC
552 Everett Ave, Suite #2
Palo Alto, CA 94301
United States
www.redhillpublishing.com

Distributed by Greenleaf Book Group. For ordering
information or special discounts for bulk purchases, please
contact Greenleaf Book Group at PO Box 91869, Austin, TX
78709, 512.891.6100.

Design by Domini Dragoone
Cover photo and interior photos by Marco Catini Photography
Archival images from the author's personal collection

10 9 8 7 6 5 4 3 2

In memory of
Joseph Patrick Hiney

Watch your way then, as a cautious traveler; and don't be gazing at that mountain or river in the distance, and saying, "How shall I ever get over them?" but keep to the present little inch that is before you, and accomplish that in the little moment that belongs to it. The mountain and the river can only be passed in the same way; and when you come to them you will come to the light and strength that belong to them.

— Mary Ann Kelty

CONTENTS

FOREWORD

creaming across the European countryside, racing in front of millions of fans on the world's biggest stage, the Tour de France is the culmination of a road racer's entire career. Success at the Tour is reserved for the best of the best of the best. Meanwhile, merely making it there is a tremendous accomplishment that only a few professional cyclists achieve. The Tour de France is euphoric and an adrenaline rush like no other; plain and simple, it's the big time.

When I first migrated to Europe to race a bike, I thought I was in pursuit of a life of glamor and fame. There is a fraction of truth in that, yet more often than not, pro bike racing is a crude and honest sport. There doesn't exist a concrete foundation with assured job security, so in the blink of an eye it can be yanked out from under you by an untimely visit to the pavement, an illness, or simply a lack of results.

The highs are high and the lows are low. Pro racing shines a glowing light on those who win consistently, but it valiantly honors those who prevail through adversity. Discovering how to pick yourself up off the ground, how to rebound from sickness, or simply how to soldier ahead through whatever roadblock you encounter — that's the crux of *Shift*.

— TED KING
Professional road racing cyclist (2006–2015)

During my early phase of recovery following the accident that provided the impetus for this book, I considered writing a book about my journey. But I never did. Instead I focused on my recovery, family, and career. Plus, I never considered myself a writer. Over time, the idea of writing a book faded.

But when I left my executive position to start Peloton Coaching, I met some wonderful people. And as it is with most introductions, they said to me, "Tell me about yourself."

After learning my story, those people encouraged me to write a book. They suggested it would be fantastic both for growing my executive coaching business and for securing engagements.

I liked the sound of that. Growing my new business and speaking about my journey seemed like a smart thing to do. So I started to write *Shift*.

I wrote some, but I got stuck. I would circle back and write some more, but I got stuck again. "Start then stuck" was my cycle for several months.

Then in March 2016 I enrolled in Seth Godin's altMBA, an intensive month-long program that was to change the way I thought about many things. I decided to make *Shift* the focal point of my altMBA experience.

The first question Seth asked us "ruckusmakers" about our endeavors was, *What is it for?* It's such a simple question. As it relates to *Shift*, it was profound.

His question helped me clarify why I wanted to share my story. *Shift* isn't about best-seller lists, making a ton of money, growing my business, or speaking engagements.

Shift is for my two daughters, Elle and Grady. They were too young to remember the time before my last bad day and the early stages of my recovery journey. They are the inspiration and motivation behind my desire to create better tomorrows.

Elle and Grady, I love you more than you imagine. I'm so proud of who you are becoming.

Shift is also for my best friend, wife, and life partner, Lynn. She has been with me through every shift, and I can't imagine my life any other way.

Lynn, I love you more each day we are together. Without a doubt, I got the best deal.

And *Shift* is for anyone looking for a new perspective that will help them become the best version of themselves.

Welcome to my peloton. Pedal fast. Ride safe.

"

SHIFT is for anyone looking for a new

perspective that will help them become

the best version of themselves.

Welcome to my peloton.

Pedal fast. Ride safe.

"

CHAPTER ONE

MY LAST BAD DAY

The truth is you don't know what is going to happen tomorrow. Life is a crazy ride, and nothing is guaranteed.

— EMINEM

It was still dark out when I put on my cycling kit that morning — my bright-yellow ONCE cycling jersey, black Lycra shorts, shoes designed to clip into my pedals, helmet, and sunglasses to reduce the glare once the sun made its appearance. It was July 11, 2001, and I had woken easily in my hotel room despite a little remaining jet lag from my flight two days before. I was excited to get in some laps before the day began.

My company was having a sales conference at a resort somewhere in the open desert between Albuquerque and Santa Fe, New Mexico — a place that felt to me like the middle of nowhere. Just beyond the resort's swimming pools and manicured golf course, I saw nothing but dry grass and desert brush in all directions.

I hadn't been looking forward to this conference. Since I had just returned from a weeklong meeting, the last thing I wanted to do was spend another week far from home, missing my wife and two young kids while I sat in another nondescript hotel conference room watching PowerPoint presentations and discussing sales strategies. Not to mention I wasn't even in sales — my department was marketing! And just as important, the Sunday after the conference, I had signed up for a cycling race, my first in years, and I was anxious to work my way back into racing shape. After several years of transition — moving to New Jersey, having children, and furthering my career — my wife, Lynn, and I had finally settled into a routine. For me that meant I could finally get back to racing.

I didn't have great expectations for my performance in the competition; I was just excited to participate. Still, I was frustrated when I learned that my company had scheduled a conference far from home right before the race. To salvage my lost training time and log some much-needed cycling miles, I decided to bike while at the conference. My plan was to wake up early each morning, before the conference began, and at the very least do a few laps around the property. I had borrowed my friend Derek McGinty's Bike Friday folding travel bicycle and had brought it with me to New Mexico.

Like the other participants, I arrived at resort the day before our meeting began, and that evening, my coworkers and I went out for dinner at a Mexican restaurant. I had what must have been the worst Mexican food I have ever tasted. The chicken enchiladas were inedible, and even the margaritas were horrible. *Where are we? What are we doing out here?* I thought to myself. I missed my family and my life back in New Jersey. We must have gotten one heck of a deal from the hotel, I figured, to come all the way out to the middle of the desert in July.

I didn't train on the first day of the conference, and the event was just what I had expected. Despite the best efforts of our meeting organizers, the material presented just didn't engage me, and judging from the glazed-over looks of everyone else in the room, it didn't engage them either. Admittedly, this wasn't new for me. I had sat through plenty of lackluster work meetings and conferences in my career. While conferences certainly weren't my favorite, I chalked them up as an unavoidable part of the job, and this one wasn't the worst. In fact, that first day, I answered some trivia questions correctly and won a book — a copy of Sun Tzu's *The Art of War*. This ancient text on Chinese military strategies is often applied to modern business management. Unfortunately, I don't have much interest in that approach. I have never thought that work should be treated as if it were war. I believe that work should be about finding victories for everyone.

That night, after a quick after-dinner drink at the bar with my colleagues, I went back to my room determined to get up just before sunrise the next day. I wanted to get as many miles on the bike as I could before the second day of the conference. While everyone else was asleep in their hotel rooms, or plodding along on the hotel gym machines like hamsters on hamster wheels, I would be enjoying the vast expanse of the New Mexican desert, the brisk morning air and bright sun on my skin.

• • •

⚙ I HAVE LOVED RIDING A BICYCLE EVER SINCE THE first time I got up the bravery to ride my little two-wheeler without training wheels. I vividly remember flying down our sloping driveway without a helmet, right into the middle of the road. To be honest, I probably wasn't going that fast, but a five-year-old's imagination and memory have powerful tendencies toward exaggeration. That said, if a car had come through, that would have been the end of me, right then and there. But I was too young to understand the danger; all I knew was the incredible joy of careening downhill on two wheels. I can still remember the feeling of exhilaration and the wind on my face.

There's something so magical about a bicycle. There's a simplicity in all those circles — the wheels, the crank, the cogs — that reminds me of da Vinci's drawings. To me, it's also functional art. I love how you use your own energy to move the wheels to propel your body forward through space. On a bicycle, you have a perspective different from what you have in a car. I love the sense of adventure, independence, and freedom that comes with cycling.

Back in the late 1970s and early 1980s, cycling wasn't nearly as popular as it is today. In the United States, bicycles were viewed as just for children, something that you used to get to and from a friend's house or to assist with an early-morning paper route. Once you were old enough to drive, a car was the respectable, adult way to get around town.

For me, that changed when I first caught a glimpse of

the Tour de France — the world's most prestigious bike race. I remember watching edited footage of that incredible race on the *CBS Sports Spectacular* on Saturday mornings. Even though they probably only showed twenty to thirty minutes of it, the Tour de France was so different than anything else I had been exposed to. I was fascinated watching those cyclists push themselves to their individual limits while using teamwork in a way that was completely different than in other sports. Soon after, in the summer of 1984, cyclists from the United States suddenly burst onto the scene, dominating the Los Angeles Olympic Games. I was sixteen at the time, and I remember watching with pride and amazement as the U.S. team took home four gold, three silver, and two bronze medals for a sport that, prior to that moment, had barely been on my radar. Two years later, American cyclist Greg LeMond became the first non-European professional cyclist to win the Tour de France. That was it — I had caught the bug. I knew I had to return to my childhood love of cycling.

I quickly became swept up in the romance and culture of this traditionally very European sport. Particularly in France, Belgium, and Italy, cycling was not only a viable mode of transportation for all ages, it was considered a serious sport. National and regional teams as well as company-sponsored teams were common, and organized races for such teams consistently drew thousands of avid cycling fans. I was entranced by the idea of teams of rugged cyclists tearing through the narrow cobblestone streets of picturesque little French villages. I loved the toughness and blue-collar-ness of it all, the camaraderie and competition. When I watched the 1979 film *Breaking Away*, about a small-town kid who becomes obsessed with Italian bicycle racing and dreams of becoming a competitive cyclist, I thought to myself, *That's me!*

My father and I shared a love of sports — playing sports, watching sports, discussing sports — but this had always involved the traditional American sports. I had spent much of my childhood and teen years connecting with my father over our mutual love of baseball, basketball, golf, and bowling. My father was even my Little League baseball coach. Suddenly, in my late teen years, I started wearing Lycra and shaving my legs. Although he never said anything, I think my father felt, at least at first, that my interest in cycling was a bit different. He, along with most Americans, didn't understand its nuances, but he was supportive of my new pursuit.

After I graduated high school in 1985, I left my parents' home in upstate New York to attend James Madison University (JMU) in Harrisonburg, Virginia, two hours southwest of Washington, DC. At JMU I pursued a marketing degree, and my free time and energy went into working on campus and starting JMU's very first college cycling team.

There, my appreciation of riding with a team and the mentality of the "peloton" grew. This French word translates directly as "platoon" in English, and it describes the main cluster of riders in a race. Prior to college, I had done much of my riding alone, except for a ride with a friend or in a race here or there. Now I experienced the upside of riding with a team. Though a peloton might seem, at first glance, to be nothing more than a bunch of individual racers each striving toward his or her own goal at the finish line, there is actually much teamwork and collective strategy involved. For example, when you are riding behind a fellow cyclist, his or her body will intercept and cut the wind resistance for you by as much as 40 percent. This tactic, known as "drafting," allows you to go just as fast as the other rider while exerting much less energy. It is a great way to save energy for the end of the race, when racers will break away from the peloton and sprint for the finish line.

When I look back on the years I raced in college, I realize that, despite being strong, I probably wasn't the smartest, most strategic racer. I tended to burn up my matches too early with ill-advised breakaways, which didn't allow for enough energy at the end, when I needed that final push. I was also too cautious. At the end of many races, things can get fast and a little rough. At times I was too timid to take the risks necessary to win because I wanted to avoid crashing. Because I played it safe, my results suffered.

I still remember those years with fondness, traveling to small towns around the region to compete in races. Racing was something I did for fun; it certainly wasn't a

"

I quickly learned the benefits of riding with a group and the mentality of the "peloton" ... Though it might seem, at first glance, to be nothing more than a bunch of individual racers each striving toward his or her own goal at the finish line, there is actually much teamwork and collective strategy involved in a peloton.

"

professional pursuit. Cycling is one of those sports that you've got to work really hard at just to be good enough to hang in the peloton. I had put myself through college with loans, and I certainly wasn't going to be able to pay them off with cycling.

When college came to a close in 1989, it was time to shift my focus and get a job. But what job? I knew I wanted to do something with my marketing degree that made a difference and helped people. With a father in sales and a mother in nursing, I chose to enter the pharmaceutical industry. This seemed a natural progression. I felt good about joining a field dedicated to providing medicine for people who need it. Yes, there is a commercial aspect to any pharmaceutical company, but there is an altruistic side as well.

Because many pharmaceutical companies hired only people with sales experience, I spent the first year and a half out of college selling copiers and fax machines. It wasn't my favorite job, but I chose to see it as sales boot camp. I learned a lot in that time, and my experience helped me land a pharmaceutical sales position in Washington, DC. I thought I had struck gold. Not only was I making good money for the time — $30,000, plus a company car — I was working for a company that was developing a novel drug to treat vascular disease, which was an issue that was important to me.

However, everything changed when the Federal Drug Administration chose not to approve the drug we were developing for sale. Because of this unexpected development, the company was forced to do some restructuring, and my entire team was downsized, me included. This was the first time I realized how important it is to differentiate yourself in the workforce, to stand out from the herd.

After trying my hand at another company for a few months, I ultimately landed a job as a medical sales specialist for a small Japanese multinational company that was in the process of opening a subsidiary in the United States.

I met my future wife, Lynn, through a personal ad I posted in 1992, not long after I had started in the pharmaceutical industry. Lynn was everything I had been looking for: a strong, independent woman "not afraid of expressing her opinion on today's events." That was the line in my ad that hooked her. We were married in 1994, and in the years that followed, we moved out of the DC area to New Jersey and the suburbs of New York City in late 1998, where I was offered the opportunity to shift from sales to marketing, and where Lynn and I started raising a family.

Those years were fruitful but stressful. A few days before starting in the corporate office in New Jersey, the vice president of the company called me and said, "You'll be working directly with me." The guy who I thought was going to be my boss unexpectedly resigned two days earlier. Suddenly, I had to take on many responsibilities of the former marketing director. All this on what was not only my first day on the job but my first day in marketing!

Ultimately, the work was interesting, and I felt passionate about our mission. Our company had partnered with a major global pharmaceutical corporation based in New York City to promote a drug that our company had developed for Alzheimer's disease. Prior to this development, there had been nothing safe and effective on the market to combat the debilitating effects that Alzheimer's disease has on memory, function, and behavior. I had seen the disease up close: my great-aunt came to live with us when I was a young boy, and she had suffered from Alzheimer's. It was scary to see. Then, after Lynn and I married, Lynn's father developed early-onset dementia, which he dealt with for about ten years before he passed away. In my job, I felt driven to help get the word out to people about their options for treatment.

Although the work was exhilarating, I always felt like I was racing to play catch-up. A typical weekday for me was packed with back-to-back meetings, and on the weekends I often had to travel for work. At home, Lynn took care of our newborn daughter, Elle, and by the time I came home from work at night, she was tired from attending to the baby all day. We would eat dinner, put Elle to bed, and I would get back on my computer, responding to emails and finishing more work. I justified this way of living by reminding myself that it was the career I had chosen, and in many ways, it was good enough.

Oftentimes, though, I felt guilty for moving Lynn up to New Jersey, away from her friends and her career in

Washington. Before we moved, Lynn had worked as the director of international programs for a trade association. It was an exciting job that required a lot of foreign travel. Ultimately, we knew it wasn't the kind of job she could do while being the kind of parent she wanted to be. Because of this, we decided that she would leave her job to focus on the family, while I would be the one to prioritize my career.

My boss at the time was also a family man, but his kids were a bit older than mine, so he would often get in to work later in the mornings and work later into the evenings, while I would arrive at work early so I could be home before Elle needed to go to bed. Early in my tenure as a marketer, my boss would come down to my office at 5:30 p.m. and say, "Let's go grab dinner and get some sushi." Then he would get caught up in important matters, and it could be another two hours before we even sat down together. This was no fault of my boss, but I felt like I couldn't say no.

On the nights when I didn't have to work late and on the weekends, it was important to me to spend my few precious moments with the family or to give Lynn a bit of alone time for herself. Because of this, my cycling time was inconsistent. My Serotta racing bike desired a little more quality time.

Our life had only started to feel more settled a few months before the New Mexico conference in July 2001. Our second daughter, Grady, was then about six months old, and our family felt complete. Lynn had made some friends — other mothers in playgroups — and I felt like I had a firmer grasp at work. Things were easing up as we settled into a routine that at last felt manageable. It was time for me to get back on the bike.

Over several weekends, I went out on group rides with local cyclists. These were humbling experiences that reminded me of how long it had been since I had been a regular cyclist. I knew I wasn't in racing shape yet, but I signed up for my first race in years as part of my commitment to get back into the sport. When that Sunday, July 15, arrived, I wanted to give it my best shot.

THE FIRST FEW LAPS AROUND THE RESORT WERE very peaceful. The sun had yet to rise, but already it was sixty degrees and beautiful. I love riding early in the morning and seeing how life wakes up around me. Since the loop around the resort's service roads was about two miles long, my plan was to throw down ten or so laps and, by the end of it, be charged up for the second day.

That early in the morning the traffic was sparse, save for a few hotel employees heading to work. Compared to the busy traffic of commuters in suburban New Jersey, this was a dream. The sun was just peeking over the Sandia Mountains in the east as I turned south for my fourth lap. Four is my favorite number, although in Japanese, it's sometimes pronounced "shi," which is also the word for death. As I navigated a particularly bendy section of the road, my blood pumped through my legs and my heart beat faster.

Then suddenly, without any warning, a huge, white SUV drifted, crossed the center line, and headed right for me. The moment was surreal. My fight-or-flight mechanisms kicked in, and what must have been seconds felt like days. I assumed that the driver would see me and veer back to his proper lane, but as he got closer, I could sense he wasn't paying attention. When he was right on me, I could see his face. He had the look of a person who had just been changing the radio station or adjusting the heat, only to look up and see a deer straight in his path. Only this time, I was the deer. I kept thinking, *This isn't happening, this isn't happening*, as my brain struggled to process what was very much happening. Finally, my flight instincts took over and I turned my bike, but there wasn't enough time. That big, white Ford Explorer came at me so fast that I couldn't react quickly enough.

I wish I could say that something meaningful flew through my mind in that instant — my life flashing before my eyes, or images of my wife and children — but the truth is, the moment was so visceral, there was no room for thought. All that I was aware of were the sounds: the whack of my body hitting the car's grill, the crunch of the bicycle under the weight of the SUV, the crack of the windshield as I broke through it, the screech of brakes as the vehicle came to a halt, and the thud of my body as I slid off the front and onto the road.

Lying on the cold desert asphalt in a pool of my own blood, I didn't even have the time to worry about my own death before I slipped away into unconsciousness.

CHAPTER TWO

IS THIS WHAT IT FEELS LIKE TO DIE?

Maybe who we are isn't so much about what we do, but rather what we're capable of when we least expect it.

– JODI PICOULT

I slowly regained consciousness as the EMTs surrounded my limp body and tried to assess the damage. They had been called to the scene not by the driver who had hit me but by the driver of the car following behind him. Luckily, the EMTs were on staff at the resort, so they arrived within minutes. Despite my fear and confusion, I was struck by their calm, patience, and professionalism. Only in their late twenties, they did their best to get the necessary identifying information from me. Back then, I didn't ride with identification. A wallet would have been too big and bulky in my cycling jersey, and products like Road ID — a personalized bracelet with name, address, and emergency contacts etched onto a metal plate — were brand new and not widely known.

As I lay crumpled on my left side, I did the best I could to explain to the medics who I was and what I was doing biking through the New Mexico desert at sunrise. However, it was clear from their responses that I wasn't nearly as coherent as I thought I was. I had to repeat myself over and over again. "My name is Michael O'Brien. I'm thirty-three years old. My phone number is . . ." But I was mixing up digits and getting the number wrong.

Top: At the accident scene, the EMTs set up a morphine drip and cover me with blankets to keep me warm and prevent shock setting in.

Above: The front grill and windshield of the SUV show the damage from my body's impact.

The police arrived next. Some were from the Native American reservation (on which the resort is located), and some were local police from the nearby town of Bernalillo. One of the police officers kept busy taking copious notes for an accident report. The police questioned the driver of the SUV, who was clearly shaken up. He had also been injured from the accident — although not nearly to the degree that I was — and had gone into shock. Some of the glass from his shattered windshield had embedded in his face. A state trooper also arrived. Although I didn't know it at the time, the reason the trooper had been called was to legally pronounce me dead on the scene.

But I wasn't dead. I was still very much alive, despite the massive and life-threatening injuries I had sustained. One clear indication of my aliveness was my excruciating pain. It was like nothing I had ever felt before. I knew I was in very bad shape. I could see on the faces of the EMTs that they were worried about my condition. But they worked with a purposeful urgency that never appeared panicked or chaotic. A couple years ago, I heard a word that describes perfectly what I imagine when I look back on this scene: *brutiful*, which is a combination of *brutal* and *beautiful*. The scene, with my body in a heap, incapable of movement, and lying in a pool of my own blood, was so brutal. Yet the way the EMTs acted, with such kindness and patience, was incredibly beautiful.

Tears rolled down my face as the EMTs wrapped me

in a blanket and set up a morphine drip to ease my pain. I was losing blood, and it was clear that there wasn't much time to get me to a hospital.

One of the EMTs tried to comfort me by letting me know they had called for a medevac helicopter to take me to the University of New Mexico Hospital. For me, however, this was the opposite of comforting. In 2001, I was still a bit of a nervous flyer. Even when I flew on a commercial airplane, I would grab my armrest at every bump, afraid of losing control. I had never been in a helicopter before, and from my perspective, they seemed way more dangerous than an airplane. "Really?" I asked them hesitantly. "A helicopter seems a little extreme." But the EMTs were insistent. An ambulance would take approximately forty-five minutes to reach the hospital, while a helicopter would only take nineteen. "We need to get you to the hospital right away because your injuries are significant," they told me. I realized I wasn't in any position to argue.

As the sun rose over the peaks of the Sandia Mountains to the east, we waited for the helicopter to arrive. Perhaps to make light of the situation, or perhaps because I was still in denial about how bad my condition was, I asked the EMTs, "How's my bike?" Perhaps you have to be a cyclist to appreciate or understand this sentiment, but we cyclists can get very attached to our bicycles. Bikes are such personal things: they can be very expensive and customized to fit a rider's needs. And this wasn't even my bicycle! It

*Top: The EMTs continue to care for me as
we wait for the medevac helicopter to arrive.*

*Above: Looking at the accident scene from behind, the SUV is
clearly on the wrong side of the road, even after the impact.*

belonged to my friend Derek. While I was truly concerned I had wrecked my friend's bike, this was simply the classic cyclist's question. If the EMTs were amused by my concern, they didn't show it. "You don't need to worry about your bike right now," they told me gently. "You gotta focus on you."

The next thought to float into my mind was, *I'm going to be late for the meeting.* Being late was, and still is, a huge pet peeve of mine, but considering the circumstances, you'd think I would have let myself off the hook. Clearly, my way of coping with the severity of the situation was to focus on minor inconveniences. I imagined everyone gathering in the conference room, wondering what excuse I would tell to justify my absence. I've heard a few creative excuses for missing work in the past, but never "I got hit by an SUV while riding my bike." But, hey, if you're going to do it, do it right!

The EMTs kept returning to my side to reassure me that help was coming and to let me know that they were trying to reach my company and my wife. I thought of Lynn, back in New Jersey with the girls. With a three-and-a-half-year-old and a seven-month-old, our family life was already demanding enough. We weren't looking to add any unnecessary drama. But I could tell by the looks of concern on my attendants' faces, what had happened that morning in New Mexico would still be a problem when I got back to New Jersey, and for a long, long time after that.

In moments, I felt incredibly lonely. While the EMTs were doing their best to comfort me, their primary concern was attending to the physical aspects of my trauma. Despite their reassurances — "The helicopter is coming Michael," "We're doing all we can" — I sometimes felt as though no one was around me. It seemed as though I was just lying on the cool desert asphalt completely alone. Despite the morphine, I couldn't move without feeling intense pain. The minutes ticked away like hours. I was fixated on not falling asleep, so I kept on telling myself, *Do not fall asleep. Whatever you do, do not fall asleep.* I worried that if I fell asleep in that moment I might never wake up again.

As I fought the strong urge to slip into unconsciousness, the severity of the situation sank in. Suddenly, a thought floated to the surface of my mind, one that had been submerged underneath all the other seemingly pressing, everyday concerns. *Is this what it feels like to die?* I thought. Lying on the side of the road, completely incapacitated by pain, while the sun rose overhead, I thought: *This is not how this is supposed to end.*

In that moment, I realized that all of these preoccupations — the bike, the meeting, the helicopter ride — were just ways of avoiding having to look at the bigger problem. They were just shiny objects. I was allowing myself to be distracted by them instead of facing my fears. I did this too often in my life. I allowed small worries to distract me from the things that really mattered. I would play small,

"

As I fought the strong urge to slip into

unconsciousness, the severity of the

situation sank in. Suddenly, a thought

floated to the surface of my mind, one

that had been submerged underneath all

the other seemingly pressing, everyday

concerns. Is this what it feels like to die?

"

letting distractions prevent me from moving forward and achieving success. Focusing on what really matters takes courage, and it takes risk. I told myself right then and there that if I lived, I would make my life different. I wouldn't allow myself to be distracted by shiny objects anymore. I wouldn't settle for "good enough."

As the warm sunlight slowly filled the sky, my ears suddenly tuned in to the faint whir of a helicopter in the distance. *At last!*

The helicopter touched down near us, and the EMTs, with their unwavering professionalism, delicately approached me. "The helicopter's here, Michael," one told me. I was relieved but still nervous about my flight.

They tried to lift my limp and battered body off of the bloodstained asphalt and onto the backboard, but it was unbearably painful. I had never experienced anything so excruciating in my life. I let out what I can only describe as the primal scream of a trapped animal. The EMTs immediately stopped what they were doing and tried to conceive of a different strategy, but the reality was, there just wasn't going to be an easy way to get me onto the board and into the helicopter. I was simply going to have to muster my strength and bear it. The second time they attempted to lift me onto the board, I silently told myself to focus. It was still incredibly painful, but the paramedics were a bit gentler this time, and together we managed to get me onto the backboard and into the helicopter.

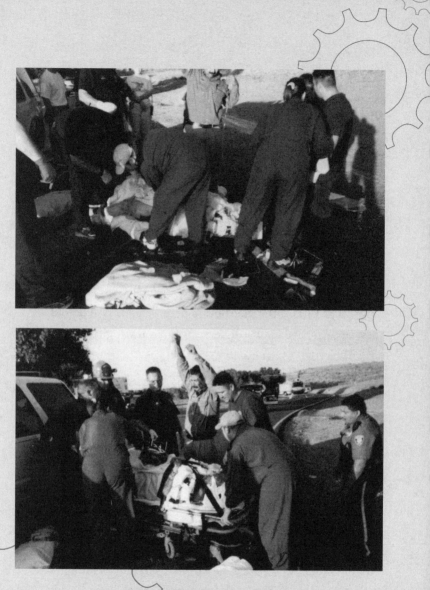

Top and above: The helicopter crew (in jumpsuits) prepare me for the flight to the University of New Mexico Hospital's trauma center in Albuquerque.

When we took off, I reminded myself that in only nineteen minutes we would be at the University of New Mexico Hospital's trauma center in Albuquerque. As the state's only level-1 trauma center, they have become, by necessity, excellent at providing comprehensive trauma care. I was very fortunate that we were so close. Imagine if this had happened in an even more remote location!

It wasn't nearly as cold inside the helicopter as it had been outdoors, and I could hear the loud hum of the blades overhead. As the pilot navigated over the sparse desert and the suburbs of Bernalillo, I focused all of my attention on the nurse sitting beside me. She had on a blue helicopter suit, with a blue helmet, big protective sunglasses, and a headset to communicate with the pilot about my condition. She was probably in her late twenties or early thirties, and she had brown hair and a very kind face, which I could see despite her sunglasses. For the next nineteen minutes, her face was my entire world. I remembered that when my wife was giving birth, she was told to focus her attention on something to manage the pain. It was true: focusing did help to mitigate my pain. After having felt so alone while waiting for the helicopter, it was comforting to have someone by my side. She kept giving me progress reports, which the pilot must have been communicating to her through her headset. She reassured me, "You're doing great. We're almost there." She could see the tears in my eyes, and she made a point to ask me questions—polite questions about

Top and above: As the EMTs wheel me on the backboard to the waiting helicopter, the accident investigation team examines the scene.

my family and where I was from. In whatever small way she could, she tried to distract me from my pain and fear.

Although no one told me explicitly, I sensed that it was still important to stay awake. As I concentrated on the nurse's face, my silent mantra became *Keep your eyes open, OB. Keep your eyes open, OB.* In my professional life, my nickname is "OB," and it's become such a part of me, it's even what I call myself. I felt that if I could stay awake, I could maintain a small amount of control over the situation. Even though I clearly didn't have any true control at all, at least if I was awake, I wasn't dead. If I fell asleep, I lost control — and if I lost control, I might die.

Among my feelings of fear and despair, another feeling also crept in: peacefulness. I used to feel so scared of death, but lying there, wrapped in blankets and strapped tightly to the backboard, things started to shift. Since that day, my understanding of death has become completely different. I now realize that it wasn't death I once feared nearly as much as it was the unknown. We cannot know what happens when we die, but eventually we all die, and we truly only have the Now. By letting go of my strong need to maintain a sense of control, I've realized that I actually have far more control over the way I live my life than I ever understood before.

As that sense of peacefulness surrounded me, we touched down on the roof of the hospital in Albuquerque.

CHAPTER THREE

MY VERY BEST FRIEND

*If you don't like
something, change it.
If you can't change it,
change your attitude.*

— MAYA ANGELOU

As the helicopter landed in Albuquerque, New Mexico, it was nearing 9:00 am in New Jersey. At that moment my wife, Lynn, was in our hot and stuffy attic spraying for ants.

Lynn had been awake since six that morning with Grady, our seven-month-old, and she had just put her down for her first nap. In between tending to the baby and getting our eldest daughter, Elle, ready for camp, Lynn had found a rare and precious forty-five spare minutes to attend to a much-needed household chore. That was what our life was like back then. We found time to do the extra things in brief windows between scheduled activities. Lynn always felt that structure helped the girls know what each day would bring, and she was great at scheduling play dates and activities for them. In just a little while, some friends would pick up Elle to carpool to a camp program for pre-schoolers, just like clockwork.

As Lynn crawled around the fiberglass insulation and air-conditioning ducts with a can of spray, she heard the phone ring from downstairs. Back then, our attic didn't have an attached, pull-down ladder. Access was just a big square hole in the ceiling, and you had to position a standing ladder below to reach it. The first time the phone rang, Lynn decided to let it go. She didn't know who would be calling her that early in the morning, and she was in the middle of a project. The second time she heard the phone ring, Lynn poked her head out of the square in the ceiling and listened as someone left a message on the answering machine — she heard only snippets, but it was enough to know that she needed to pick up the phone.

She did, and one of my colleagues in New Mexico told her what had happened. However, the details were murky; he said only that I had been in a bike accident and recommended she get on an airplane to New Mexico as soon as possible. "Really? He's crashed before," she protested. "I'm really very busy. I've got a seven-month-old and a three-and-a-half-year-old. I'm still breastfeeding. Just send him back home." With that, she hung up the phone.

A few minutes later, the phone rang again. This time, it was another senior colleague, whom Lynn knew personally. "Lynn, you really should come out," he insisted. He admitted they didn't know very much at that point, but they had heard I had broken both legs. Lynn still wasn't convinced it was a genuine emergency, and again, she said no. As she told me later, she thought: "That's bad, people break their legs, but I can't just pick up my whole life at this moment. We don't have family around here. I can't just go running out the door and leave my kids with my mother."

He wouldn't take 'No' for an answer. "Listen, you really need to come out here," he implored her. "We don't know what's going on, but you really need to be here." He told her the company would fly her out, and that by the time she arrived, I would already be in recovery. Finally, Lynn agreed. He suggested that Lynn pack for a week given the uncertainty of my injuries.

Just as Lynn got off the phone, our friend Dave arrived with his daughter, Courtney, to pick up Elle for camp. Events were moving so quickly, Lynn said she felt like a "deer in the headlights." She froze trying to figure out how to manage all the logistics. Luckily, Dave calmly told Lynn, "Pack your bag, and pack a bag for Elle, too. After camp today, Elle is going to come and stay at our house, and you're not even going to worry about it." Today, Dave and his wife, Colleen, are two of our closest friends, but at the time, we hardly knew them. The fact that they didn't hesitate to watch our daughter for an indefinite period at a time of crisis was one of the most generous and compassionate acts of the whole ordeal.

With that, Lynn quickly packed all the necessary bags, said goodbye to Elle, gathered up Grady, and took a car to the airport.

• • •

AT THE TIME OF MY ACCIDENT, LYNN AND I HAD been married for seven years. We met in 1992, when we were both living in the Washington, DC, area. I posted a personal ad in a weekly local paper, although I didn't have high hopes for any great results. I'd moved to the area a few years before for work, and I hadn't yet found a person I wanted to have a meaningful relationship with, but it seemed worth a shot. I still remember the ad:

> SWM, 24, 6 ft. 2 in., 190 lbs, college educated, professional, into cycling, running (10Ks), hiking, HFS [the local alternative radio station], going out, staying in, ISO [in search of] SWF, 23–25, intelligent, athletic, humorous, and not afraid of expressing her opinions on today's events. Into having lots-o-fun with greater possibilities.

Although I cringe now when I read that last sentence, I have to hand it to myself — that ad did the trick! A few days after the paper came out, I got a handful of strange responses, including one from a woman who lived in a halfway house, had just sold all her possessions except for her bicycle, and thought this connected us. However, I also received a response from a young woman who seemed to fit the description of what I was looking for exactly.

The first time we spoke on the phone, Lynn and I talked for an hour and a half. We only got off the phone when she had to meet a male friend from college who was in town. I couldn't believe it! By the end of the conversation, I was jealous of this friend, even though I hadn't yet even met Lynn in person!

We spoke again on the phone before agreeing to meet for a date. Lynn waited nervously by the window for me, wondering what kind of person would show up. This was in the days before social media and smartphones, so she couldn't Google my name and find out what I looked like. Lynn told me later that when she saw me walking down the street, she said to herself, "I hope that's him!" She was both relieved and excited when I turned and walked up her walk.

I wanted to go somewhere familiar and relaxed, so I took Lynn to my favorite place, Austin Grill, a little Tex-Mex place in Alexandria, Virginia. Their frozen margaritas were excellent, I could practically recite the menu backward and forward, and all the bartenders knew me well enough to call me "OB." We had a great time. Lynn was so fun and easy to talk to. We discovered lots of common ground, and I loved learning about her life, her interests, and her career.

By her twenties, Lynn was already highly accomplished. After earning a bachelor's degree in Russian studies and pursuing a master's degree in Russian language and literature, she used her Russian speaking abilities to snag a prestigious position with a trade association managing new development in what was then still the Soviet Union, as well as overseeing other international programs. She would be in Spain one month, then Egypt or China the next.

It wasn't hard to fall in love with Lynn. She was so dynamic and alive. I had never met someone who was so warm and affectionate and, at the same time, who had such tenacity and drive. She had this incredible way of making things happen. I remember traveling with her one time after we were married but before we had kids. At the airport, Lynn dropped me off to deal with the check-in process while she parked the car. There was some complication with exchanging our tickets, and the woman at the desk was having difficulty sorting it out. I said to her, "Listen, my wife is parking the car. You can deal with me or you deal with my wife. I advise you to deal with me." Literally two minutes later Lynn walks up, takes in the scene and asks brusquely, "What's going on? Is there a problem?" I just looked at the woman and shrugged my shoulders. "I told you," I said.

Lynn changed somewhat after spending three years at home taking care of our two kids. She remained as focused and driven as ever, but she realized she wanted to use those skills in a different way. Lynn became fascinated by the birthing process, reading books and taking education classes for both of our daughters' births. When she reentered the workforce, she knew she wanted to spend her time and energy supporting other women who were giving

It wasn't hard to fall in love with Lynn. She was so dynamic and alive. I had never met someone who was so warm and affectionate and, at the same time, who had such tenacity and drive. She had this incredible way of making things happen.

birth. So Lynn decided to train to become a doula: a person who provides support and education to families through the many stages of the birth process. In fact, Lynn's first training session was scheduled to begin about two weeks after my accident. It would be another year before Lynn would be able to finally start her doula training program. She was about to have her hands full with all the caring and supporting she could muster.

LYNN'S CONTINENTAL AIRLINES FLIGHT TO NEW Mexico had a layover in Houston, where she called the hospital to check on my status. Someone informed her that I was still in the operating room. At the time, she didn't think anything of it, telling herself, *His surgery must have been delayed because something really bad happened to someone else.* Not unlike my own reaction immediately after the accident, Lynn's reaction was to avoid acknowledging how serious things were; she didn't even consider that the "really bad" thing might have happened to me! On the second leg of her flight, when the flight attendants passed out freshly baked macadamia nut cookies, she tucked one away in her bag. She figured by the time she arrived, I would be in recovery and glad to enjoy a sweet treat.

My company arranged for a car to drive Lynn from the Albuquerque airport to the hotel, and they also arranged for a nanny to help care for Grady. The nanny had been told about my accident, and that I might not survive, so she was quite surprised when Lynn showed up at the hotel and seemed in no rush to get to the hospital. Rather than being distraught, Lynn took the time to give the nanny painstaking instructions on how to care for our seven-month-old daughter.

At the hospital, Lynn found it quite difficult to get any clear information on me and my condition. Because I didn't have any ID on me, I still hadn't been officially identified. A few colleagues had come to the hospital, but hospital policy was that only family members were legally allowed to identify a patient. Thus, I had been designated "Trauma Patient Mango." No matter how many times Lynn insisted that she was the wife of Michael O'Brien, that name didn't have any significance to the hospital staff. Today, we hold a special place in our hearts for mangos, but in the moment, Lynn didn't find this nickname particularly charming. She wanted answers!

Eventually, Lynn learned that I was still in surgery and that I had been under for eight hours. For the first time, Lynn began to realize how serious my condition was. Of course, none of staff knew exactly what had happened to me, nor did they know anything about the progress of my surgery. Finally, after another hour or so of waiting, Lynn marched up to the desk outside of the operating room, and in typical Lynn fashion, she proclaimed, "I don't care if it's the person picking up the sponges off the floor. I want

Above: Before being identified by Lynn, I was "Trauma Patient Mango".
My mom created Mr. Mango Head to brighten up my room.

somebody in that room to come out here right now and tell me what is going on with my husband!"

A nurse coming off his shift in the OR heard this and approached Lynn. "Your husband's been in a very bad accident," he told her. "We did the best we could, but the next forty-eight hours or so are going to be critical." This floored Lynn. Until that moment, she had maintained the belief that my injuries, though troublesome, were certainly not life-threatening. In the face of such trauma, she realized what a sweet but naive gesture it had been to stow that little macadamia nut cookie in her bag for me.

Eventually, Dr. Mark Langsfeld, the vascular surgeon, came out of the operating room and gave Lynn the full details on the extent of my injuries. I had broken my right shoulder, right femur, and right tibia; I had shattered my left femur; and I had severe lacerations to my femoral artery. I required a transfusion of thirty-four units of blood (roughly the equivalent of fourteen liters of blood), and I required fasciotomies: cuts in the connective tissue just below the skin to relieve pressure from swelling. The surgeon told Lynn that they wouldn't know for several days whether or not my leg could be saved. He also told Lynn that, had I been ten years older or not in such good health, I would have bled to death before even arriving at the hospital.

I was unconscious when I was wheeled out of the OR and into the intensive care unit, and Lynn realized there

"

I had broken my right shoulder,

right femur, and right tibia; I had

shattered my left femur; and I had

severe lacerations to my femoral

artery. . . . The surgeon told Lynn that

they wouldn't know for several days

whether or not my leg could be saved.

"

was nothing she could do for me. So she went back to the hotel, fed Grady, and tried to get some sleep. Now that she understood the severity of the situation, she knew she was going to need all her strength to handle whatever complications arose tomorrow, and in all the days to follow.

Lynn slept fitfully that night. Finally, at 3 a.m., she called her best friend in Boston. "Michael's been in an accident," she confided. "He's in critical condition in an ICU, and he may lose his leg — or worse."

July 11 had started like any typical day, but by the end, it had shifted like no other.

CHAPTER FOUR

FIGHTING FOR LIFE

We can't escape pain; we can't escape the essential nature of our lives. But we do have a choice. We can give in and relent, or we can fight, persevere, and create a life worth living, a noble life. Pain is a fact; our evaluation of it is a choice.

— JACOB HELD

From my perspective, the rest of July 11 was hazy at best. After the helicopter landed on the roof of the University of New Mexico Hospital, I was put on a stretcher, wheeled to the elevator, and taken down to the trauma room. My whole body was still strapped tightly to the backboard, and a massive plastic collar supported my neck, so I couldn't really get a clear view of what was happening. Although I could see only the ceiling above me, I could hear all the action, and I could sense the energy of the room. Medical practitioners buzzed all around me, moving with the synchronicity of a team. It was a very purposeful, organized chaos, and it reminded me of a scene out of the television show *ER*, only this time I was living the show, not watching it.

Into my narrow field of view appeared the face of Dr. Robert Schenck, the chief of the orthopedic department, who would be my trauma surgeon that day. Immediately, I got a good feeling about him. He reminded me slightly of John Wayne. As he looked down at me on the stretcher, he said, "It's a pleasure to meet you, despite the circumstances." We shared a laugh about the intensity of the moment and the unfortunate situation that brought us together. He reassured me that they were going to get me into surgery as soon as possible, right after they took an X-ray and an MRI. I instinctively knew that I was going to be in good hands, and I remember feeling relieved and hopeful as the anesthesiologist put me under. There was no reason to fight to stay awake any longer, so I drifted off. I wouldn't remember a thing for the next five days.

The surgery lasted for approximately twelve hours. The damage was so extensive that even in all that time they were able to operate only on the left leg, which had sustained the most extensive injuries. The first order of business was to attend to the bones, starting with my femur, which had shattered above my knee. Because of all the swelling, it was difficult to determine how long to make my leg. Dr. Schenck did the best he could to make my left leg the same length as my right, but to this day, it is about a half inch shorter.

After several hours nailing the fractures together, Dr. Schenck was just about ready to have my leg stitched up when he felt my foot and realized it was ice cold. There was only one explanation: an injury to my vascular system. He immediately called in a vascular team, headed by Dr. Langsfeld, to perform another operation on my left leg. As the doctors described it to me later, when my left femur shattered, it was like a bomb going off inside my leg. Shards of bone went in all directions, cutting into the femoral artery. Luckily, because I was still young and athletic,

I had a strong peripheral blood supply, so the vascular surgeon was able to perform a femoral popliteal bypass surgery: this complicated procedure involved removing a great saphenous vein from my right thigh and grafting it into my left knee and thigh to act as an artery instead. (A vein brings blood from the organs to the heart to oxygenate it, while an artery brings the oxygenated blood from the heart back to the organs. Pretty much the same structure, but the opposite job.) Had I not been an avid cyclist, it's very possible that I wouldn't have been able to undergo this complicated surgery. "Being a cyclist, you had tremendous fitness, strong heart and lungs, and you also gave me great protoplasm," Dr. Schenck told me later. "You brought a lot to the table."

It was ironic, in a way, that while riding a bicycle was what nearly killed me, it was also the thing that saved my life and leg.

Although I didn't know it at the time, I was also exceptionally lucky that Dr. Schenck had been on call that day, and that he was the one who came in as my orthopedic surgeon. Raised in the West and trained as an orthopedic surgeon at Johns Hopkins University in Baltimore, Dr. Schenck had gained experience with shock trauma while working in San Antonio, Texas, from where he had just relocated. As a sports surgeon and a trauma surgeon, he was truly in his prime. In orthopedics, Dr. Schenck says, they joke that there are certain trauma centers like University of

"

Had I not been an avid cyclist, it's very possible that I wouldn't have been able to undergo this complicated surgery.... It was ironic, in a way, that while riding a bicycle was what nearly killed me, it was also the thing that saved my life and leg.

"

New Mexico (UNM) and San Antonio where you "drink out of a fire hose" when you're on call. He had already seen about ten cases involving a similar kind of medial femoral condyle fracture and quadriceps tear. Part surgeon, part cowboy, Dr. Schenck knew how to be aggressive with trauma management while, at the same time, attending to the whole patient. With injuries as severe as mine, there is an 8 percent chance that the leg will have to be amputated if it is not reconstructed within the first six to eight hours. I had been hit at six in the morning, so there was no time to lose. Had another surgeon been on call that morning, they very well may have made the difficult choice to amputate my leg. Because of his skill and experience, Dr. Schenck was committed to saving my leg. The choices he made under pressure that morning were big and bold, and while there were risks involved, his expertise and his training couldn't have been better suited to the task.

After the surgery, I was taken to the intensive care unit (or ICU) to rest and recover. They hooked me up to a respirator, multiple IVs, and an oxygen tank. My right leg was put in traction. It was hoisted up by pulleys that connected to a pin above my kneecap, while my left leg was heavily bandaged and equipped with a drainage portal.

My whole body was covered in lacerations and bruises, including glass fragments that had embedded in my right cheek when I broke through the car's windshield. My face and body were massively swollen from the transfusion of

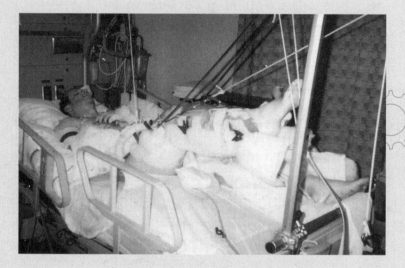

Above: Early days of my recovery at the University of New Mexico Medical Center, when my right leg was in traction.

blood and plasma, which is also injected into the blood-stream to help the body absorb and process the new blood. I was so unrecognizable that when Lynn showed one of the nurses a photograph of me on our wedding day, which she kept in her wallet, the nurse couldn't believe it was the same man as the one who now lay in bandages in front of her.

Through the next few days, I was given a cocktail of serious medications to mitigate the pain and keep me in a resting state. Having never been much of a drinker in college, and having never even tried drugs, a little went a long way. I was really out of it. In my hazy, drug-induced state, I tore at my IVs and my nasal oxygen supply. I must have been a dream for the nurses, who had to restrain my arms to keep me from pulling out the crucial, life-saving equipment. Once, Lynn got permission from the nurses to take my hands out of the restraints while she was visiting with me, and of course, the minute my hands were freed, I immediately began to grab at all the equipment. As she tells the story, she gently tried to persuade me not to fidget, saying, "Don't do that, Michael." To which I responded, "Fuck you! You can't tell me what to do!" Not only was I far from having a "sailor's mouth," Lynn knew that I would never curse at her in real life. Because of this, Lynn found it all terribly amusing. I have no memory of anything from those days.

It turned out that, in my foggy state, I had all kinds of great advice and business wisdom to impart. I once told

Lynn to buy stock in Amazon.com, which was fifteen dollars a share back then, and another time I interviewed her for a job at my company! She walked into the hospital room, and I greeted her with, "I'm Michael O'Brien. It's a pleasure to meet you. Thanks for coming in for the interview." I even sat up in the bed and shook her hand as I said, "So what makes you think you're qualified for this job?" Finding all of this quite charming, Lynn played along. At the end of the interview, I told her that it might be awhile before she heard about the next steps. I had been in a very bad accident, after all.

Because of my bizarre behavior, Lynn kept asking the nurses if they were positive that I didn't have a brain injury of any sort. They reassured her that the CAT scans and MRIs had come back negative. Although I had clearly suffered a concussion, I was lucky to have escaped more serious brain injuries because I was wearing my Giro cycling helmet that day. I always wore my bike helmet when I rode, as a safety precaution, but until that day in July, I had never really put its life-saving abilities to the test. Now that I had, was I grateful for my bike helmet.

A few days into my recovery, while still in a delirious state, I managed to burble something that, in retrospect, seems especially fateful. As Lynn sat beside my hospital bed, I told her, "Find David; follow David Kolb. He is our leader." Although she didn't know who David was,

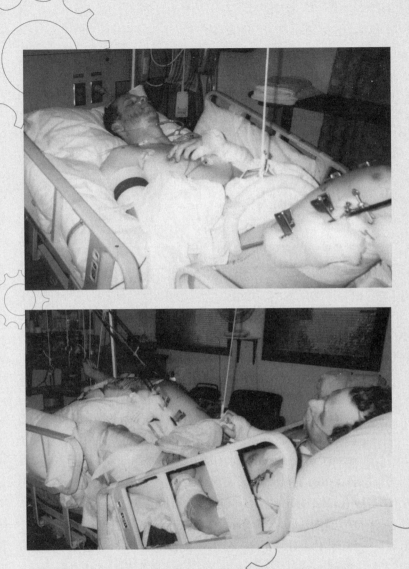

Top and above: Resting in the ICU, heavily bandaged but with the facial lacerations from the windshield glass clearly visible.

Lynn didn't press me on what I meant; she simply wrote down the name, and when I was more lucid, she asked me to explain.

David was the first executive and team coach I had ever met. Back then, in 1996, I didn't even know that "business coach" was a career option. My company had hired David as a coach to strengthen our leadership and partnership abilities for our copromotion when we first started selling the new Alzheimer's drug. David had a few years on me; he was about six feet tall and wiry from his hiking and cycling pursuits. He had a quiet, spiritual wisdom with the kind of crunchy-granola energy that you would expect from someone who lived in Freeport, Maine, the home of L. L. Bean. He always seemed so comfortable with his style and in his own skin. This was a far leap from how I felt at the time, wearing a formal suit and tie and subscribing to the "fake it until you make it" philosophy of external calmness, even when I felt so much pressure and internal churn. Unlike so many other leaders I have encountered in business, David wasn't obsessed with always being right. He had a real Zen-like approach to work, and I got the sense that he had been through a lot in his life that had made him wiser and more resilient for having experienced it. His strategies for finding different approaches to problems so that everyone could win, as well as his message to focus on the present moment, really resonated with me. I loved his spirit and I loved his ideas, and the work we did with David created a beautiful partnership. At the time, I hoped that one day I would be able to embody David's calm demeanor and generous nature. But I suppose those weren't the only things about him that I wanted to emulate. Although it would be many years until my own professional career transitioned into executive and team coaching, I suspect that my wheels were already turning subconsciously in that direction. And it was all because of David Kolb.

After about four days of drug-induced haze and uttering incoherent gibberish, I finally came out of the woods. I was moved out of the ICU and into the orthopedic wing of the hospital. When I finally regained some clarity it was the middle of the night, and I was all alone in my single room. As you can imagine, it was hard for me to take in my new surroundings and circumstances. My left leg was wrapped up, and I had no idea what kind of condition the leg was in underneath all those bandages. My right leg was strung up in a contraption that reminded me of an erector set. As for my upper body, I was covered in bruises and cuts, with a beautiful black-and-blue mark on my forehead from the impact of my head against the windshield. As I tried to move myself into a more comfortable position, I noticed how painful and difficult it was to move my right shoulder. I suspected it was broken. While the pain was significant, it was nothing compared to what I remembered experiencing before going in for surgery. I used my call button to summon the nurse and asked her how to mitigate the pain. She directed my attention to the button by the side of my bed, which would release pain medication intravenously into my blood. Good to know! I had a feeling that I would be pushing that button repeatedly. It felt good to give myself a few pumps of medication to ease the pain and to feel a slight sense of control over my own life again.

When Lynn arrived that morning, she was so relieved to find me more like my old self — or, at least, alert. While the scene wasn't necessarily something out of a Hollywood movie, I was incredibly happy to see her. Before losing consciousness, I had felt so alone, but now having Lynn by my side and feeling her loving understanding and reassurance was heaven sent.

For Lynn, the moment when I asked her about the girls was a huge relief. Until that moment, I hadn't mentioned anything about the family in my semiconscious babbling, and she had been concerned that I wouldn't remember who I was or our life before the accident. For her, it was a turning point to finally know for certain that I hadn't suffered any serious brain injuries.

Dr. Schenck came to visit me, and he gave me a rundown on the specifics of my accident and the surgery that had followed. He explained that the two massive incisions in my left leg were fasciotomies. If medical descriptions make you queasy, you might want to skip this next part. My first fasciotomy was a small six-inch cut into the fascia layer of the skin on the outside of my left calf. My second fasciotomy was a massive gash stretching from just above my ankle to all the way above the knee on the inside of my left leg. Although they were gruesome to look at, they were necessary to minimize the risk of compartment syndrome, when the swelling after an injury leads to the inhibition of blood flow and severe tissue damage. To decrease the risk of infection, these wounds needed to be unwrapped, cleaned, drained, and re-dressed frequently.

Dr. Schenck also broke the news to me that I still needed to undergo a second surgery to address the tibia and femur fractures in my right leg. Now that I was cognizant, they scheduled surgery for 5 p.m. the next afternoon. This meant no rest for the weary. Since I couldn't eat or drink anything (except water) for twelve hours prior to surgery, I was starving by the time 5 p.m. rolled around, which was ironic because until then I hadn't been hungry at all.

Compared to the twelve-hour marathon of the first surgery, the second surgery was a relatively quick, three-hour sprint. Dr. Schenck and his team repaired the breaks in both my right tibia and my right femur. I now had matching internal femur rods stretching from my hip to my kneecap in both legs. The right leg also required six screws, about half of what the left leg needed. I couldn't help but notice that the equipment they used on my legs looked very much like something from aisle eight at Home Depot. I guess attaching bones to one another isn't that different from attaching two pieces of lumber.

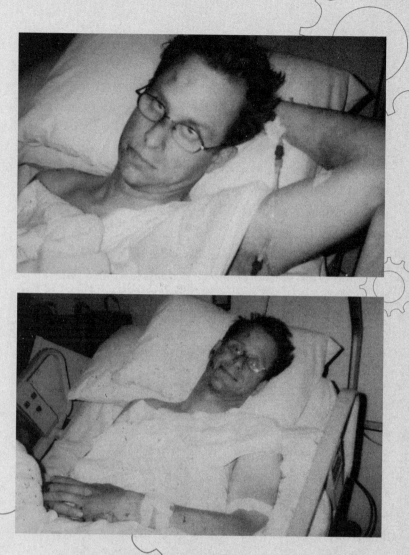

Top and above: In the ICU I frequently felt angry, frustrated, and
scared, though I did my best to put on a happy face for visitors.

After my second surgery, there was nothing left for me to do but settle in for the long, slow process of recovery. At this point, I had no idea what exactly that would entail or how long it would take. I just knew that I was taking my first step on an uncharted and unfamiliar path. Luckily, I didn't have to go on this journey alone. With Lynn by my side, I could rest easy knowing that she would take care of all of the logistics, so I could focus all my energy on my recovery. I have never been so grateful for Lynn's "get it done" attitude. She kept notebooks full of details from all the people she spoke to about the accident and my health. She talked to people who had been at the scene of the accident, including the sheriff, the police, and the EMTs. She spoke to those in charge of my care — Dr. Schenck, Dr. Langsfeld, and all of the nurses at the hospital as well. At the same time, she was responsible for informing our wider community of friends, family, and colleagues about the accident and then managing the outpouring of support she received via emails and phone calls. She was fantastic. I was so comforted to have her as my advocate, my partner, and my rock. Without her as the main partner in my peloton, I don't think I would have made the recovery that I did.

It was right around this time that I received an email from a fellow cyclist who had also suffered a terrible injury just a few weeks earlier.

July 16, 2001
Subject: Former D20 rider seriously injured in NM

Michael:

Stay strong, try to remain positive, and be patient. I'm sure your family will give you great comfort and support. All the prayers and all the worlds of encouragement that you get from family and friends via emails, letters, cards, phone calls, and personal visits will be very helpful during your recovery. I know this because I just spent almost two weeks in the ICU and TTU at Lehigh Valley Hospital after hitting a wall at the velodrome. I am at home recovering from multiple head, facial, neck, and upper spine injuries. I should make a full recovery over time. It is just difficult dealing with the day-to-day healing process; most of your strength seems to go into being patient and remaining positive. My wife, children, family, and friends, especially in the cycling community, have been a tower of strength for me. My injuries are superficial compared to what they could have been. Countless people have told me that they were praying for me at the time of the accident and afterward; I am thankful that God spared me from more serious injury. I realize that your injuries are serious and painful, but we both can be thankful that our injuries were not more serious and disabling.

All the best in your recovery!

Reading this email made me feel so much less alone. At the hospital, when visiting hours ended, it sometimes felt like I was truly all by myself. But it was comforting to be reminded that I was in people's thoughts, and that many people, certainly many cyclists, had gone through a similar ordeal. Even now I love a good recovery story. They give me a feeling of spiritual connection, not just to people who have also experienced such trauma and recovery, but to all people who have suffered.

CHAPTER FIVE

GESTURES OF KINDNESS

The real winners in life are the people who look at every situation with an expectation that they make it work or make it better.

— BARBARA PLETCHER

Life in the orthopedic wing was full of surprises. After my surgery, I moved to a different room, this one with a roommate. Although we were only ten or fifteen feet apart, we never talked. While he seemed like a nice, quiet fellow when we were alone in the room, I got an altogether different picture of him when the nurse came in to question him.

"Do you drink?" she asked.

"Yes," he answered.

"Do you smoke?"

"Yes."

"Do you do drugs?"

"Yes."

As he went down the list of all the drugs he took, I thought to myself, *Holy cow! This guy is a hot mess*. But apparently he was quite popular: his phone rang off the hook, day and night. His ringtone was the theme song to the TV show *The Simpsons*, which I found amusing at first, but after the fiftieth phone call, it really started to get on my nerves.

Also around this time I started to notice the sound of the medevac helicopter touching down on the roof of the hospital. I realized that each time I heard that familiar whir of propellers, it meant that someone like me, with injuries as life-threatening as mine, was being brought into the hospital. That sound never failed to make me sad, as I always thought their situation might not turn out as fortunately as mine.

Despite my luck, I was still having trouble seeing the forest for the trees. I really thought that I would make a speedy recovery. I couldn't wait to be healed and return to regular life. I'd obviously missed the cycling race the Sunday after the New Mexico conference. But before my accident I also had listed another race as a goal: at the end of July in Frederick, Maryland. I had enough sense to know that I wasn't going to be able to ride by then, but I was convinced I would be in good enough shape to watch the race. Lynn, in her infinite wisdom, told me that I was absolutely crazy. She knew I would be in no condition to travel in a car or stand and watch the race in a mere few weeks. I suppose I was being delusional, but at the same time, I had never experienced anything like this before. I really had no idea how long the road to recovery would be. I was still chasing the shiny objects, distracting myself with plans and schemes, rather than focusing on the difficult reality of the present moment.

While I was busy making unrealistic plans for the future, my vascular team, along with the nurses, was diligently checking my lower legs to make sure the blood was flowing properly. Unfortunately, they found that my pulse was still quite weak in my left foot, even though my pulse was quite strong at the site of the bypass in my left thigh. If the pulse in my foot didn't improve, this could potentially lead to further complications that might require additional surgery or even an amputation.

The game of "find the pulse" caused me a lot of worry and anxiety. For some doctors and nurses, locating my pulse was easy; for others, it seemed like searching for a needle in a haystack. In order to make it easier for those who struggled, the doctors and nurses would draw an X on my leg with a Sharpie marker, which indicated my pulse like the bounty on a treasure map. Eventually, I realized that the accident had compromised the nerves in my left leg. At the beginning of the pulse checks, I couldn't feel when someone touched the bottom of my left foot, but thankfully, over time, the sensation returned. Also around this time, I began to feel the effects of neuropathic nerve pain, which occurs when damaged nerve fibers send incorrect signals to the brain. One minute I would feel fine, and the next minute a lightning bolt would hit my foot, shooting intense pain up my leg and curling me up in the fetal position.

These setbacks often put a serious damper on my mood. I had told myself that life would be different if I survived on that morning of July 11, but I didn't expect it to be harder. I didn't recognize that I was going through

The doctors were pleased with my recovery, but the life they depicted for my future was too full of compromises and limitations. . . .While I did the best I could to put on a happy face, the truth was, I frequently felt angry, frustrated, and scared.

the five stages of grief: denial, anger, depression, bargaining, and finally acceptance. The doctors were pleased with my recovery, but the life they depicted for my future was too full of compromises and limitations. I worried about reduced mobility, having to get knee replacements, and diminished athletic ability. My new physical complications were difficult to process. While I did the best I could to put on a happy face, the truth was, I frequently felt angry, frustrated, and scared.

To make matters worse, I felt sick and nauseous much of the time, and the food at the hospital was horrible. At times, I would lift the little dome over my tray and gag at just the smell of mystery meat, limp veggies, and applesauce. I even threw up a few times because of it. I'm sure my medication influenced my nausea, but my state of mind certainly didn't help. The nurses warned me that if I didn't eat, they would have to give me a feeding tube, since calories and protein were absolutely necessary to fuel my recovery. I felt like a stubborn child bitterly chomping on his vegetables so his mother would stop nagging.

On days when I had my wounds re-dressed, I was given morphine to deal with the pain. I was brought down to the first floor of the hospital to work with the burn unit physical therapist, Yvonne. She was an angel. Her job was to attend to the bandages on my fasciotomies, which had to be drained and re-dressed daily because of seepage and leakage. This was intensely painful, of course; these were open wounds. But Yvonne was adamant about giving me the best kind of care, and she worked at a steady but deliberate pace, making sure that everything was done by the time the pain medication wore off. Not only that, she brought me donuts from the first Krispy Kreme store in Albuquerque. Since the store had just opened, people would wait in line for up to two hours just to get their donuts. Maybe Yvonne never waited in line that long, but her consideration and generosity stunned me. Plus, the simple carbs and sugar were exactly what my body craved. No, it wasn't the diet of champions, but a calorie is a calorie, and I was desperate for something to stay down. My roommate's *Simpsons* ringtone must have foreshadowed the donuts to come.

A few days after I was moved out of the ICU, Lynn entered my room and informed me that my parents were there. It was astonishing news. The last time my mother had been on an airplane had been almost twenty years before, when I was in seventh grade. Although she would deny it, saying, "I just didn't like to fly on airplanes because I didn't want to go anywhere," I think the truth is that my mother, like many others, and like myself to a lesser degree, was fearful of flying. The fact that she overcame her fears to get on an airplane and fly to New Mexico was a clear indication of just how worried she was about me. We were all worried, even when we pretended not to be (and I was doing the most pretending of all), but my parents' presence was a clear indication of their love. I had grown up in a caring household, but not necessarily one with a lot of physical affection or saying "I love you" all the time, so it meant a lot that my parents came to the hospital to express their love and concern. It helped me understand more clearly how dedicated they were, and are, to me and our family.

My mother had been a nurse, and when she had children she switched her schedule from the day shift to the overnight shift so she could take care of my sister and me. To this day, I still don't know how she did it. She got by on four hours of sleep some days, and she spent her waking hours tending to either her children or her patients.

My father also had a very strong work ethic. It's one of the things I cherish about him, and it shaped who I am today. As a salesman at Seagram's and then in the moving industry, he taught me a lot about customer service. I admired his ability to connect with others and go beyond his customers' expectations. Both of my parents worked really hard to make ends meet, so that their children could go to college and have a good life.

In the hospital, my father sat by my bedside as he asked me questions and talked, but I got tired very easily. Any conversation that lasted more than half an hour made me fall asleep. It's ironic, but when you lie down all day long, you get tired. Not to mention the laundry list of medications I was on, including Percocet; these didn't help me stay awake, either. My father did his best to keep me engaged, talking about sports and making conversation.

My mother went right into "nurse mode." She wanted to know all about how I was doing and what kind of care I was getting. At the time, the hospital nurses were particularly concerned with my bowel movements — or rather, my lack of bowel movements — and my mother took it upon herself to be equally concerned.

"Michael, did you move your bowels today? Do you feel like you have to go?" became a frequent line of inquiry by my mother and others.

Joking aside, I knew why it was important. I wasn't eating properly, the drugs were slowing down my metabolism, and if things got impacted, there could have been trouble of a new kind. Nevertheless, it was still humiliating. Any time I would feel something stir and call for the bedpan, all my family members and the staff would become eager with anticipation. Stop the presses — he's about to poop!

Getting on the bedpan was no small feat. It was difficult just to sit up, considering that my broken shoulder couldn't bear the weight of my body, and I couldn't use either of my legs for leverage. Scaling that small plastic bedpan, only about six to eight inches high, was about as difficult as mounting a horse without any stirrups. Once I had finally positioned my body on top of it, the nurses would draw the curtain around my bed to give me some privacy. But with my wife, my parents, and the nursing staff waiting just on the other side of the curtain, it didn't feel very private! My mother would lovingly call from the other side of the curtain, "Are you done yet? Are you done yet, Michael?" The pressure to poop was enormous! I assured them that when something happened, they would be the first ones to know. I wasn't going to be keeping any secrets from them!

I must have had five or six false alarms. We resorted to a variety of solutions, including a medical laxative, but at the end of the day, good old-fashioned warm prune juice did the trick. To me, in that moment, prune juice was my idea of a good time.

I've never thought so much about pooping in my whole life. When you're a parent, you make a big deal out of your baby's poop. "Yay! Look who pooped! What a good girl! Who's a pooper!" Whole books have been written on the subject of babies and pooping. The ability to toilet yourself is one of those thresholds that mark the shift from a baby to a child. But then we reach a certain age and the topic becomes taboo. It becomes disgusting to talk about poop. It's only when we become sick or very old that we openly discuss the subject again. Now I was getting a glimpse of what old age might be like. It might include dementia, or wearing a diaper, or having other people attend to your bowel movements. The helplessness and the lack of dignity that can come from not being able to toilet yourself can't be

"

While I definitely struggled with feelings

of dependency and vulnerability,

I also deeply appreciated having

people around who helped me through

these physical necessities in a caring

and respectful way. . . . I don't know

how much nurses get paid, but I am

confident in saying it isn't enough.

"

underestimated. It can plant the seed of doubt that you'll ever be healthy enough to take care of your basic bodily needs again. It makes you wonder if you're going to be dependent on other people for the rest of your life.

When I finally did have a bowel movement, I had to call a nurse in to clean me up because I wasn't able to clean myself. While I definitely struggled with feelings of dependency and vulnerability, I also deeply appreciated having people around who helped me through these physical necessities in a caring and respectful way. The nurses at the hospital, both male and female, managed to make the occasion as dignified as possible. I don't know how much nurses get paid, but I am confident in saying it isn't enough. Yes, doctors are awesome; the incredible life-saving work they do should be praised. But the nurses in the hospital run the show. They're the ones who take care of you, feed you, bathe you, and give you your medication. The people who choose to become nurses, who dedicate themselves to providing for people at their most vulnerable, are doing the work of saints. They have become an important part of my peloton, and I will never forget the care of those nurses who attended to me in New Mexico. Life looks different from the top of a bedpan, and it's not pretty.

AFTER A FEW DAYS, MY PARENTS RETURNED TO upstate New York, and Lynn continued to attend to Grady and to me, research the accident, and make phone calls and emails on my behalf.

Lynn did an excellent job handling the outpouring of concern and support, which came in from all directions. Rather than respond to each person individually, she soon discovered that it made more sense to send out one big email letting everyone know of my progress. Her emails became an important bridge to our community, and they reflected a sense of optimism for my recovery and eventual return home.

Here's the first of Lynn's recovered emails to our family and friends. She had written a few others before July 19, but they were lost to cyberspace's black hole.

July 19, 2001
Subject: Michael update

Hi Everyone,
We're all doing well, especially Michael! The next paragraph has some marginally graphic descriptions in it, so if you have a weak stomach, skip it!

He is recovering from his 2nd surgery since July 11th. This one was on his right leg on Monday. He's doing very well. The orthopedic team is very happy with their work and his progress; they consider the bulk of their job to be done. The vascular team has him on their "service" now, so they are responsible for him. The injuries to his artery were very severe and life-threatening so they need to be watched closely. The worst part of his day is the bandage changes in the morning. The wounds on this left leg are still open. When the femoral artery was lacerated, it bled very heavily into this leg and into the tissues, which then swelled. They also swelled because of the fluids administered during the initial surgery and due to the massive blood transfusions he received. Because of the swelling, he received two fasciotomies — these are slits into the skin that relieve the pressure that can build up and eventually restrict blood flow in the leg, in his case. These fasciotomies are still open wounds.

He has reduced the pain meds he is taking to almost nothing, remarkably. After his 9 a.m. dressing change this morning, he didn't take anything else all day. He said his legs felt achy but didn't hurt. Amazing!

I'm so grateful to all of you for the unbelievable outpouring of support you have continued to show to Michael, to me and the girls, and Megan, our babysitter, too! How lucky we are to have all of you in our lives and helping us in this time.

All of you have asked what you might do for us. I have given this a lot of thought as I have whiled away the hours in the ICU and now in the hallways of the hospital. Three things keep coming to me:

1. ALWAYS wear your bicycle helmet when you ride, no matter where you are going or how safe you perceive it to be. It goes without saying that your kids should be wearing theirs, too.

2. Sometime in the next year, if you are physically able, please give blood one time. We're so grateful that others gave blood so that Michael would have some when he desperately needed it in surgery.

3. Consider donating platelets. This process is called apheresis. I actually used to do it, so I know what it's about. It's a rather time-consuming process, but those who receive your platelets will be so glad you have done it. Michael received four units of platelets in the ICU, and we're so glad that someone gave of themselves in a way that eventually benefited Michael. During apheresis, blood is removed from one arm, the platelets are spun out, and the blood (without platelets) is put back in your other arm. The process takes about two hours. I used to just rent a movie and watch it while donating platelets.

Hope to see you SOON!
Love, Lynn

Ultimately, the outpouring of support that Lynn and I received was really surprising to us. On the one hand, some people we had expected to offer support were noticeably silent or absent. As we expected, many of our close friends reached out to ask how they could help. Then, a few people truly surprised us by going above and beyond anything we could have expected.

In other words, I learned some important lessons about how people respond to a crisis:

> Some people you expect to show up, don't.
> Some people you expect to show up, do.
> Some people surprise you by showing up in unexpected ways.

While I was in the hospital, I couldn't help but feel resentful toward the people in the first group who didn't show up. Their actions (or lack of action) really surprised and disappointed me. Several of my colleagues at the meeting in New Mexico did not come by the hospital to visit. I would have thought they would have come simply as a kind gesture on behalf of my company, and when they didn't, this hurt me.

Since then, I've realized that people don't always know what to do in these situations, and they can become overwhelmed themselves. They don't mean to be hurtful or cruel. Facing someone in my kind of critical physical and

❝

People don't always know what to do in

these situations. . . . Facing someone in

my kind of critical physical and emotional

condition can be difficult, scary, and

uncomfortable. People come face-to-face

with their own mortality. They worry that

they won't do or say the right thing.

❞

emotional condition can be difficult, scary, and uncomfortable. People come face-to-face with their own mortality. They worry that they won't do or say the right thing. As a result, they stay on the sidelines. But the longer they remain silent, the harder it is for them to say something. It's a powerful loop.

Even strangers have the power to hurt you. At one point, Will Miller, a close friend and fellow cyclist, updated the cycling community in the Washington, DC, area about my accident. However, reading his bulletin, some thought I — not the driver — was on the wrong side of the road. Rather than offer unwavering support to an injured cyclist regardless of the circumstances, some people took the opportunity to be critical. One stranger responded by posting the online comment, "Serves him right." Of course, most of the people in the cycling community sent emails and letters of support, but I found it hard not to focus on the less-kind, anonymous internet responses.

Today, I realize it was selfish to let myself become frustrated with people who disappointed me and to let my hurt feelings and negative energy dampen the tremendous amount of positive energy I was receiving from other people. Today, I choose to focus on those who did reach out. And I like to think that even those who didn't contact me still thought of us and our situation and sent good wishes, even if they didn't know how to express them. I prefer to feel gratitude for their unspoken thoughts, and I thank them.

Of course, I'm also forever grateful for the many close friends who truly showed up for us, offering their love and assistance. Dave and Colleen gave great care and attention to our eldest daughter, Elle. Our friends Kathy and Ben did the same. They all were so supportive of our family.

On occasion, support arrived in really lovely ways and from unexpected people. One of my company's representatives, who lived in New Mexico, heard about my accident and came and sat with me for an afternoon. At that point, I was still pretty spacey, but he demonstrated his care and support by talking with Lynn.

Another unexpected and special form of support during my recovery occurred back in New Jersey. Lynn's friends from her "Mommy and Me" playgroup came together to hold a prayer circle for me. It wasn't a religious ceremony, but it was spiritual. I was so moved when I heard about it. They didn't have to do it — there were plenty of other things they could have done with their lives that day — but that's what they chose to do.

When I look back on my experience today, those are the things I focus on.

✿ WHEN PEOPLE ARE IN TROUBLE, WE MAY THINK that they are so consumed with their own problems that they don't notice anything else. But take it from me, they notice which of their friends show up and which don't. As

I learned firsthand, in the absence of any contact, it's easy to let the mind roam to the dark conclusion that others don't care. Today, my advice is, if someone you know ever needs help or support, just reach out. Take the person to lunch, make a phone call, or even send an email to say, "I don't know what kind of help you need right now, but I'm thinking of you, and I want you to know that I'm here for you." Even small gestures go a long way.

Another way people can be of service is to give blood. As Lynn mentioned in her email, giving blood is a great way to help anyone in need, friends and strangers. Prior to my accident, I never gave blood. I told myself I was scared of needles, which was a very convenient excuse. What I learned from my accident is that most pain is temporary. You can do amazing things when you move past your fears and focus on the needs of others. The pain from a needle will pass, and by giving blood, you help save someone's life. My life was saved because others donated blood. These complete strangers are now part of my peloton. As a result, I now try to give blood on a regular basis. I feel the need to pay it back and pay it forward. Although my feelings about needles haven't changed much, I do love to help save lives. That love is more powerful than my fear.

And one last piece of advice: If you happen to find yourself in the position of being the one needing help, do yourself a favor and accept it. All too often, when people ask how they can support us, we say, "I'm fine, thanks for

"

If you happen to find yourself in the

position of being the one needing help,

do yourself a favor and accept it. . . .

Accepting help is a sign of respect for

the person offering it, and it benefits us

as well. It's good karma for everyone.

"

asking." So others do nothing because the person in need was too proud. Accepting help is a sign of respect for the person offering it, and it benefits us as well. The help could be something little or something big; it doesn't matter. We all need a little help to move forward sometimes, so when it's offered, accept it. It's good karma for everyone.

CHAPTER SIX

FLYING PRECIOUS CARGO

Optimism is the most important human trait because it allows us to evolve our ideas, to improve our situation, and to hope for a better tomorrow.

— SETH GODIN

After a week in the hospital, Lynn and I were anxious to return home and reunite our family. Although Grady had come to New Mexico with Lynn, I wasn't allowed to see her. Hospital policy didn't allow babies into the intensive care unit or the orthopedic wing. While we understood and respected this rule, it nevertheless put a strain on Grady, Lynn, and myself.

At least Grady was with us: our three-and-a-half-year-old, Elle, was still being cared for by friends in New Jersey. Still, we were very fortunate. She spent the first week with Dave and Colleen, who had picked her up for camp that fateful morning. After a week, Megan, our go-to babysitter, agreed to move into our house to take care of Elle at home. By then, Elle was actively missing her mom, dad, and sister, in addition to her routine. Until that week in July, Elle had never been away from her mom and dad for more than a few hours at a time. Then, one afternoon on the phone with Lynn, Elle gave the first indication that she knew this wasn't one extended playdate. "When are you and Daddy coming home?" she asked.

As the days went on, her worry became more apparent, and I found myself worrying as well. Was our normal family gone? Who was I now that I was hurt? I knew that the "me" that Elle was asking about was the old version — the "me" before July 11. I had no certainty of what the future "me" was going to be.

Elle wasn't the only one urging me to come home. Our entire community, our peloton, on the East Coast was eager to have us return. Although I was getting world-class care in New Mexico, some of our friends believed that East Coast hospitals were better. You know East Coasters: to them, New York is the center of the world, and a place like New Mexico might as well be a foreign country. Friends would say to Lynn, "You've got to get him out of there. You've got to get him to a New York hospital." I tried to explain that my doctor was trained at Johns Hopkins in Baltimore, but they wouldn't take no for an answer. Still, the issue wasn't quality of care. The truth is, the road to my recovery was going to be long. It only made sense to get the difficult step of returning home over with and out of the way, so I could begin to heal in all ways: in my body, in my life, and with my family.

However, getting back to New Jersey wasn't as simple as we had hoped. Making the arrangements for the trip back turned out to be a daunting, monumental project. The first order of business was to find a facility in New Jersey to admit me. This was easier said than done, considering the severity of my condition. In addition, I didn't really have a primary care physician at the time. I had been a healthy young man who had never had much need for a doctor. Now I did. It would have helped immensely to have had a physician advocate on my behalf with hospitals as we tried to find one that would take me in my condition. Without an attending doctor to admit me, no hospital wanted to take on my case.

As Lynn reported back to me on all the dead ends and fruitless efforts, I feared I would be stuck eating Krispy Kremes in Albuquerque forever. In retrospect, this was obviously an irrational fear. The New York area is loaded with hospitals.

Eventually, we remembered that our neighbor, Stephanie, was a plastic surgeon at Hackensack University Medical Center, which is a Level-1 trauma center. Stephanie lived a few houses down from us. Although we didn't know her very well, we would often say hello when walking our dog by her house. Lynn reached out and asked for her assistance, and fortunately, Stephanie agreed to help us out. She contacted a primary care colleague, Kathleen O'Hara, who agreed to be my admitting physician. (As a plastic surgeon, Stephanie didn't have those privileges.) I was accepted into Hackensack University Medical Center.

The next plan of action was to figure out how to get me there. As you might imagine, a private flight for a physically incapacitated man and his family is quite a costly endeavor. For this, we were at the mercy of the insurance companies, and Lynn fought like a trouper to make sure I got adequate treatment. However, they would only offer to pay for a ticket on a commercial flight. Can you believe it? The insurance company wanted me to book a flight on Continental, connect in Houston, and just cruise right into Newark. I couldn't bear any weight on my legs, had limited function in my right arm, and had open fasciotomies, yet somehow they had decided I was healthy enough to take an airplane like a normal, healthy person. It was frustrating, especially since they claimed to be "in it for the patient." Clearly, the insurance companies were in it for the money, and the insurance business is a gamble: sometimes you make money and sometimes you lose it, and they were losing a lot of money on me. In the end, my employer saved the day and offered to pay for an air ambulance back to New Jersey.

On Saturday, July 21, we left the University of New Mexico Hospital, and our departure was bittersweet. I said my goodbyes to the nursing staff with admiration, gratitude, and even a tear or two. I told them that I hoped to return again soon for a more joyful visit. Unfortunately, Dr. Schenck was away at a conference on the day of my departure, but before he left, we had made a point to say goodbye. He had wanted us to stay a bit longer so he could be there when we departed, but the desire to return to our daughter and our home in New Jersey proved too strong.

We had been told we would be flying

in a converted private jet. As we drove

to the airport, I pictured a luxurious

jet with big, comfortable leather seats,

shag carpeting, and perhaps even

cocktails and gourmet food. I was

stoked that we were going to live like

rock stars, even for just a few hours.

I had been given some medication in anticipation of the trip, the first painkillers I had taken in a few days. Perhaps because of my constipation or my worry that I would become dependent on them, I was determined to get off the pain meds. I didn't like how they made me feel, and I was afraid of being controlled by them. Still, I was having a lot of pain, particularly neuropathic pain in my left leg, so when the medical team offered me medication for the flight, I decided to accept it.

Although the transit between the hospital door and the back of the ambulance was brief, it was pure delight to feel and breathe fresh air outdoors for the first time in ten days.

I had never heard of an "air ambulance" before, but we had been told we would be flying in a converted private jet. As we drove to the airport, I pictured a luxurious jet with big, comfortable leather seats for Lynn and Grady, shag carpeting, and perhaps even cocktails and gourmet food. I was stoked that we were going to live like rock stars, even for just a few hours. But as the ambulance stopped on the tarmac by the plane, my dreams of a G6 were quickly dashed. Instead of a luxury jet, it was a tiny, nondescript airplane — nothing but a small tube with two big engines attached to it. Yes, it was a private jet, but not the type I had imagined. For the occasion, I had worn my tie-dyed Ben and Jerry's shirt that said, "If it's not fun, why do it?" On the tarmac, looking up from my stretcher at that pint-size airplane, it suddenly felt like an odd fashion choice.

To get me into the airplane, my team had to lift me, tilt me, and twist me all around. I was still strapped onto a backboard, so this was more than a little challenging. Once inside, there was barely enough room for my stretcher, Lynn, Grady, and my nurse, Rocky, who were pressed up against the curved walls of the plane. Lynn and Grady sat in seats by my feet at the rear of the plane, while Rocky sat beside me. Rocky was a huge, muscular man with a bodybuilder's physique. Even within the confines of that metal tube, he was awesome. He monitored my blood pressure, vitals, and general comfort throughout the flight.

We made a short layover in St. Louis, Missouri, to refuel the plane. It must have been one hundred degrees or hotter on the tarmac. As Rocky, the pilots, and Lynn and Grady left the plane to use the restroom and grab something to eat, I stayed in the plane, since I was still strapped to the backboard and hooked up to a catheter. Although they left the air-conditioning on for me, it was still hot as Hades. I was relieved when they returned to the plane, ready to take off again — and with a delicious turkey sandwich for me. It was the best-tasting meal I had had since my accident (not counting my Krispy Kremes!).

Six and a half hours after leaving Albuquerque, our plane touched down at Teterboro Airport in New Jersey, a

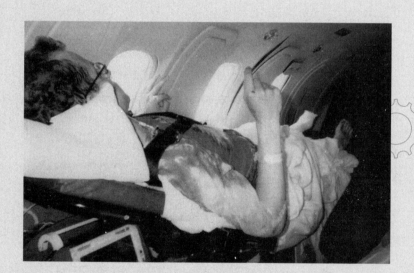

Above: Flying home from New Mexico to New Jersey, and it's definitely not first class.

small airport that often services high-level corporate executives and celebrities in the New York City area. Finally! A little rock star treatment! As we disembarked the airplane, my ambulance was right there, waiting to take me to Hackensack University Medical Center.

At the airport, Lynn was greeted by her friend Kathy, who had offered to pick up Grady and our bags and take them to our home. Lynn accompanied me in the ambulance to the hospital and helped me get admitted. She then took a taxi home to pick up the girls and return to the hospital. At this point, I got an idea. I asked Lynn to go pick up a peanut butter protein smoothie from Jamba Juice, which she could bring back to the hospital for me. Jamba Juice had just arrived on the East Coast, and I knew there was one in the Whole Foods near our house. After nearly two weeks of deprivation, I wanted to indulge a craving.

Looking back, though, I now realize that those two weeks were also, strangely enough, a whirlwind of self-involvement, in which I didn't really stop to consider how events were impacting those around me. I made my Jamba Juice request without considering what this would mean for Lynn. While this might not normally make me a contender for the "worst husband of the year" award, the fact was, I knew better. Many people have since told me that self-involvement is a normal response for people in my situation, but I believe that we are at our best when we put others first, even when we are in great need. Nevertheless, Lynn agreed to my request, and we parted ways at the airport.

Once at Hackensack University Medical Center, I discovered that the doctors didn't trust the X-rays that had been taken in New Mexico. They required a whole new set of X-rays in order to admit me into their hospital. Not only that, I also had to go through the whole ritual of telling all the medical experts about my case, and speaking to the attending physician, before I could get a prescription for pain medication. They wouldn't give me any meds until they had a full record of my health. After the long and arduous day in the airplane and then the X-rays, examinations, and interviews at the hospital, I was not in good shape. I was grimacing and sweating, and though I was stubborn about not wanting to take any pain medication, I knew that I needed it badly in that moment. I was about to see Elle for the first time since my accident, and I didn't want to scare her. I didn't want this to be the "me" she saw, laid up in bed, sweating bullets, and in terrible pain.

Lynn returned to the hospital with Elle, seven-month-old Grady, and the peanut butter protein smoothie. However, Elle insisted upon bringing it to me. Lynn cautiously reminded her to hold it with great care and not drop it. That Jamba Juice was nearly as big as Elle. Of course, Elle agreed, but a three-year-old's best laid plans often go awry. Thirty-six ounces of protein-powered smoothie hit the hospital floor before she even made it to my room. It just wasn't meant to be! When Elle came in she looked up at me with her big, beautiful eyes and said, "I'm sorry, Daddy!" For a moment, I was deflated, then we were soon all laughing about it and agreeing that it was a fitting end for such a day. The Jamba Juice didn't matter. Instead, we were thrilled to be back in New Jersey and together as a family.

Besides, I was confident there would be another Jamba Juice in my future.

CHAPTER SEVEN

FIGHTING AGAINST REALITY

The world as we have created it is a process of our thinking. It cannot be changed without changing our thinking.

— ALBERT EINSTEIN

Hi Everyone,

Michael, Grady, and I are back in New Jersey. We flew back yesterday (Saturday) via Air Response air ambulance. The plane was tiny (my friend said it was smaller than our minivan) but it did the job. Michael has been admitted to Hackensack University Medical Center in Hackensack, New Jersey. We had hoped to have him in Englewood Hospital, which is smaller and closer to us, but since the fasciotomy wounds on his leg are still open, the doctors in New Mexico encouraged us to place him in a higher-level trauma facility. Hackensack is pretty state-of-the-art.

Michael's health continues to improve. He can now lift both legs by himself, at least a little bit. He is doing exercises for the right leg and right arm already. The swelling that was around his right elbow has all but disappeared, as have most of his bruises and abrasions. He looks pretty good!

He is in pretty good spirits, mostly just bored and tired of eating hospital food. He is only being medicated when it's time for his wound dressing to change; otherwise, he's not in pain. The doctors are confident that he will be out of the hospital by the end of the week. The only reason he is in the hospital is because of the open wounds. We hope they will be closed by Wednesday, but the surgeons have not been to visit him yet. Then, he will enter a rehab facility. I am looking into those tomorrow and hope to have him placed shortly.

Many people have continued to ask, "What can we do to help?" and "Is there anything that Michael needs?" Michael wanted me to pass along to everyone that, rather than flowers or gifts for him, and for those among you that are needle-phobic and therefore not too keen to donate blood or platelets, perhaps you might like to make a small contribution to the Lifeguard Memorial Fund. Lifeguard is the air transport company whose helicopter brought Michael to the hospital. If he had been transported by ground, I don't like to think of what could have happened.

Lastly, we continue to be grateful if you just keep us in your thoughts and prayers. Take good care.

Love,
Lynn and Michael

IT WAS GREAT TO BE BACK, AND WE WERE IN REL- atively good spirits. However, Hackensack University Medical Center was an adjustment for me. It was larger and much busier than the hospital in New Mexico. The majority of patients came in for surgery, stayed a few days, and then left. Most of my roommates cycled in and out in just a few days. I was certainly in the worst shape out of all the patients in the orthopedic wing of the hospital; nevertheless, I tried to remain optimistic that I, too, would be leaving quite soon. The plan was simply to come in, have the fasciotomy and skin-graft surgery, then move to a rehabilitation hospital.

There was just one complication. During our "luxury" airplane trip, I had developed a blood clot. This wasn't expected, but it wasn't particularly surprising, either. Considering that my vascular system wasn't pumping as heartily as it normally does, and I had been strapped to a stretcher for six-plus hours, my body wasn't able to circulate my blood in an optimal way. A blood clot is a serious problem, so the doctors quickly attended to it. I was given a blood thinner, Lovenox, which was difficult to manage. It took multiple blood tests just to get the dosage right.

Then, in addition to my blood clot, I developed a new complication: a bacterial infection in my fasciotomies. Although I can never know for sure, I believe this most likely occurred because of my change of "scenery." In Albuquerque, the cleaning and wound care I received each day was far better. At Hackensack, the nurses appeared overworked and understaffed. Their relationships with their patients seemed more transactional than personal. It was hard to blame them. Patients came in, had their procedures, left, and were never heard from again. Who has time to invest in a relationship that won't last? It's no different than in any other aspect of our lives. We rarely take the time to pause, listen, and invest. Although I didn't fault the nurses for their proficient but sometimes brusque care, the infections in my fasciotomies made me wish that this hadn't been the case.

To make matters worse, I didn't see eye to eye with my new orthopedic surgeon. He seemed self-involved and spoke in a very abrupt way. I didn't fully trust him, and I dreaded his visits when he made the rounds. I got the sense that he thought I was a lost cause, and he didn't want to invest the time and energy it would take to make me well. In all my years working in health care, I have never understood physicians with a lousy bedside manner. It's as if they don't understand that their focus should be on the patient and not on their own ego. I missed Dr. Schenck, his social graces and warm personality. But I had no choice. I had to live with who I had been given. I had no relationship with any other doctor in the Hackensack orthopedics department.

One bright note was that my nursing aide was incredibly attentive. She was responsible for cleaning my bed and attending to my body: giving me a sponge bath and dressing me. Considering the medications I was on, the view from the bedpan wasn't pretty, but she handled it with compassion and managed to keep my dignity intact.

While I waited for my fasciotomy surgery, I began physical therapy. At first, it didn't go so well. We started with the right leg, as it was in considerably better shape than the left (relatively speaking). Lying on my bed, I was instructed to put my leg in a machine used for a technique called "continuous passive motion" (CPM), which slowly brings a greater range of motion to the leg and strengthens the muscles. My leg was strapped securely into the machine while it cycled through phases of flexion and extension. Eventually, I was able to transition from exercises done lying down into exercises from a seated position, and I would sit in my wheelchair while the physical therapist manipulated my leg. Oh mama, just getting into the wheelchair was so painful. My right shoulder still couldn't bear much weight, and my legs were almost useless for leverage. It took me about ten minutes just to figure out how to move from my bed to the chair.

Once in the chair, the real pain began. The physical therapist would try to flex my right leg. At first, this motion was gentle, but soon it became more aggressive. It was during one of these sessions that I suddenly heard a pop, which is never a good thing in physical therapy, I thought. The pain was unbearable, and I was overwhelmed

I had resisted using medication, and I was really struggling to cope with the pain of rehabilitation. I used alternating techniques of distracting myself and focusing on the pain, and it's hard to say which approach was more helpful.

with nausea and drenched in sweat. We later learned that the pop had created a massive scar knot that, to this day, I can still feel under the skin of my right thigh.

After the infamous "popping" session, I had trouble trusting my physical therapist not to hurt me. This mistrust made me tense, and in turn, this tension made flexion and extension difficult. I had resisted using medication, and I was really struggling to cope with the pain of rehabilitation. I used alternating techniques of distracting myself and focusing on the pain, and it's hard to say which approach was more helpful.

With all the complications I was having, the hope that I would be in and out of Hackensack in a matter of days faded away. Between the blood clot, the infections in my fasciotomies, and my slow responsiveness to physical therapy, it looked like I was going to be there at least two more weeks. It was so disheartening. Even though another facility awaited me after this one, I was so eager to just get home to heal with my family.

Although I continued to get top-notch medical care, my time at Hackensack wasn't exactly pleasant. The environment at the hospital made it almost impossible to get any sleep. From my bed, I could hear the televisions in other rooms at all hours. Not only that, but the minute I would drift off to sleep, the nurse would come by to check my vitals. She was just doing what she was supposed to, but I couldn't help wishing that her common sense would tell her to let me sleep. Instead, I spent my days and nights in a dozing state, never quite asleep nor awake. This made my interactions with visitors quite difficult. I was grateful to have friends close by who could visit me, but I was feeling angry, worried, and fearful. With difficulty, I put on a happy face for my guests and pretended to be chipper, but though pleasant, these interactions would often leave me exhausted.

THE TRUTH WAS, I WAS STILL BITTER. I WANTED revenge on the man who did this to me. I wanted to take something from him the way he took something from me. From what I knew of him, he didn't have much insurance, and he had very little in the way of material possessions. During the first weeks of my recovery, I wasted a lot of my time and energy concocting half-baked plans for enacting vigilante justice.

Many friends would say, "You're so lucky," or "God was looking down on you that day, Michael." Even though I knew they were trying to be helpful and optimistic, I had trouble seeing the silver lining.

I wanted to say, "You know what? God missed it. He could have been looking down about fifteen seconds sooner. He was having his latte, reading the paper, and he missed it. If I had been lucky, then the time to be lucky would have been about twenty seconds *before* the SUV hit me." Instead, here I was, laid up in bed, my legs barely functional, shoulder broken, feeling positively awful, looking and smelling worse. I couldn't sleep, and when I did sleep, I had nightmares — something I had never really experienced before. It was always the same dream: I was being chased by something, only I didn't have any legs. Right before the thing would get me, I would wake, panicky and drenched in sweat. The nurses would come in and have to explain to me all over again what had happened and why I was in this condition.

It was no wonder I felt afraid. When I thought of what lay ahead of me, all I could see was a lifetime of being dependent on other people. The doctors did their best to give me a picture of what life might look like in the future, but they tended to be pragmatic, if not a little pessimistic, and it was very disheartening. They warned me that the life I had enjoyed before the accident was inevitably going to be compromised. They asked questions about our shower and toilet, suggesting that we might want to get it renovated to be more handicap-accessible. This information hung over me like a big dark cloud. I didn't want to hear it. This wasn't the way my life story was supposed to be written.

I didn't feel lucky at all. I felt wronged. What was completely lost on me was the fact that I was still alive, that I had avoided any traumatic brain injury, and that I was able to see and speak with my wife, daughters, family, and friends.

"

I didn't feel lucky at all. I felt wronged.

What was completely lost on me was

the fact that I was still alive, that I had

avoided any traumatic brain injury, and

that I was able to see and speak with

my wife, daughters, family, and friends.

"

Lying in a hospital bed alone at night, my mind would wander to questions of identity. If I was going to be dependent on other people for the rest of my life, what kind of person could I hope to be now? What kind of executive? Father? Husband?

At work, I was a leader. It was my job to solve problems, not create them. Not being physically capable in the way I used to be threw all of the cards up in the air. I worried I wouldn't be able to contribute to my company in the capacity that I had before.

As for my family, being with my children made me aware of how they saw me as a father and a caretaker. I wanted to be a certain kind of dad: an active dad, the kind who gets down on his hands and knees to play, the kind who is athletic and plays sports with his children as they get older. I certainly didn't want to be limited to cheering my daughters from the sidelines.

As a husband, I worried what kind of life I could still offer Lynn. I know that when you get married, you pledge to stick to it "in sickness and in health," but in truth, few believe that they will become a caretaker for their partner. It's something that happens to other people. The thing is, it was happening to us. The words "I love you" were suddenly being put to the test.

• • •

THROUGH ALL OF THESE STRUGGLES, LYNN DID her best to remain optimistic. She has always rooted for the underdog and has a way of seeing the best in people. She didn't want other people to worry about us, and she did the best she could to "put on her game face" when connecting with friends and writing email updates. But underneath it all, the "fake it till you make it" attitude took its toll. There was a lot of pressure to keep everything together. And to complicate matters, while I was at the hospital in Hackensack, Lynn required a root canal. I guess misery loves company. Since she was still breastfeeding Grady, she did it without Novocain. Boy, she is tough.

Around this time, I started thinking about what it meant to accept help when people offered. Oftentimes I would say, "No, no, that's okay, I've got it." But as time went on, it became clear that there were things that I really did need help with — simple things like clean shirts to wear for rehab or DVDs to watch in my hospital room. Once people knew how they could help, most did in fact step up to offer it. It reminded me of cycling in a peloton, when you draft off someone and it makes it so much easier to ride. I felt like I was drafting off my friends, and it made the experience of being in the hospital so much easier.

At home, people would leave bagels and orange juice on the counter or milk in the refrigerator. If Lynn told someone she was in need of anything, they would bring it over right away or offer to lend a hand.

At the hospital, the standard cafeteria fare was vastly improved by our friends, who made sure I got a delicious meal every now and then. Two particularly memorable meals were brought by my good friends Jani Hegarty and Will Miller.

As soon as we touched down in New Jersey, Jani was on a mission to help. Like Lynn, Jani is a woman who knows how to get stuff done. I met Jani through work, but now I got to know the personal side of her. She knew that the food at Hackensack, while better than the hospital in New Mexico, still wasn't cutting it. The smell of my meals under those domed serving trays made my stomach queasy. Given my blood loss and open wounds, I needed iron and protein more than anything. I told Jani this when she asked what she could do to help, and it wasn't long before Jani brought over an eleven-ounce steak filet with spinach and potatoes from Ruth's Chris Steak House. I will never forget that meal, as it was the first truly great meal I had had since my accident, and it was filled with love and care.

Another great meal was provided by my dear friend Will Miller. Will had been the one to inform our fellow cyclists in the DC area of my accident, and he had been a constant source of support throughout this ordeal. On the phone with Will one day, I casually joked that I could really go for a burrito from Burrito Brothers, one of my favorite local spots on Capitol Hill that was famous for their "California-style" burritos. My usual was a "super spinach

Although they weren't that expensive in the grand scheme of things, these acts of giving were completely selfless. It is so uncommon to be given something with no expectations of anything in return. . . . it's such a wonderful reminder of the importance of having good relationships and true friendship in your life.

burrito." You can imagine my surprise when a week later I received a FedEx package with not one but three super spinach burritos from Burrito Brothers inside.

The meals that Jani, Will, and others provided were delicious and desperately needed to fuel my recovery. But my friends gave me far more than just a meal. Although they weren't that expensive in the grand scheme of things, these acts of giving were completely selfless. It is so uncommon to be given something with no expectations of anything in return. That's true giving. When it does happen, it's such a wonderful reminder of the importance of having good relationships and true friendship in your life. You can't have success without it, no matter how independent you might think you are.

Finally, the day came for my fasciotomy-skin graft surgery: July 31. Dr. Cohen, my neighbor who had been instrumental in getting me admitted to Hackensack University Medical Center, served as my fasciotomy skin-graft surgeon. In order to cover my fasciotomy, she harvested a four-by-twelve-inch patch of skin from my left hip and stretched it in a machine to make it large enough to cover my open wounds. I was amazed at how much the skin-grafting procedure was similar to sewing a patch onto an old pair of jeans. When it was over, my leg was bandaged up with a tube to drain the fluid. Stephanie, who is more accustomed to doing cosmetic plastic surgery, did an excellent job of making the skin graft look nice. The grafted section doesn't look exactly like natural skin; it looks like a patch, which I happen to think is pretty cool.

I have never been so happy to see a wound heal over. There was no sign of infection, and my body responded well to the surgery. One down side, however, was that the area on my hip where the skin had been removed was intensely painful. It felt like the worst road rash I had ever experienced in all my years of cycling. There was a raw, burning sensation that made it difficult to roll onto my left side, making it even harder to get comfortable than before. Even though I knew it was just another pain I had to overcome, I was also becoming desperately tired, so I decided to use pain medication so I could finally get some sleep.

As my body healed slowly, I was allowed outside for short "wheels" around the grounds, with Lynn pushing me in my wheelchair. Even though she only wheeled me out as far as the front of the hospital where the cars pulled up, it was so nice to get some sunshine and breathe fresh air again.

A few days after my fasciotomy surgery, Lynn wrote this letter to our community, to let them know how things were progressing:

August 4, 2001
Subject: Michael update

Hi everyone,

I wanted to make sure I had all the latest info before sending out another email update on Michael.

The surgery on Tuesday went very well, as well as the surgeons had hoped. The plastic surgeon performed skin graft surgery to cover/close the three open wounds on his left leg. The dressings have remained in place since the surgery and will be changed today for the first time. This will give the doctors a chance to see the work and verify that the grafts are "taking."

Michael is feeling good since the surgery. The closed wounds do not hurt him, although what is referred to as the donor site (where the skin was harvested for the grafts) is rather painful. He said it feels like road rash or a bad sunburn. He keeps it exposed to air as much as possible, and they bring in a sun lamp and shine it on the area a few times a day to promote drying and healing. The downside to the surgery has been that he has been bedridden ever since. He and I were getting spoiled with our daily walks (in the wheelchair) outside to get some fresh air and a bit of sunshine. We're hoping to resume that later today, once the dressings have been changed and the surgery sites have been checked.

He has continued physical therapy on the right leg, although at a reduced rate. Some bone has apparently calcified in that femur (a result of the break and surgery), which has caused him some pain in the area. His doctor ordered X-rays to confirm that a bone shard had not become lodged in the muscle — we were relieved to learn that it wasn't the case. He just has to work through the calcifying discomfort and strengthen the leg. The plan is still for Michael to leave the hospital (yeah!!!) on Monday, August 6, for the Kessler Institute for Rehabilitation. We decided on the West Orange location, which is their main facility. The patient population should be a bit more compatible with Michael, and since he will probably be there for three or more weeks, that is important. The drive is a bit longer for me, but still doable. I had been making two trips to the hospital daily, one long visit for me and a short visit with the girls, but that was getting to be too stressful for all of us. We cut the visits with the kids to once or twice a week, two days ago, and plan to continue that at Kessler. Of course, visits at Kessler will be planned around Michael's physical and occupational therapy schedules.

Michael's spirits are good and we are all looking forward to moving to the next step — rehabilitation. It's amazing that three weeks ago Michael was in the trauma intensive care unit in Albuquerque, and now we're looking forward to leaving the hospital and heading to rehab!

Michael is really grateful for the support and love you have shown in so many ways: phone calls, cards, emails, packages, DVDs, and of course the countless prayers, well wishes, and thoughts that are being channeled his way each and every day. Thank you all so much for everything.

Love, Lynn

CHAPTER EIGHT

MIND OVER MATTER

The greatest discovery of all time is that a person can change his future by merely changing his attitude.

— OPRAH WINFREY

After my fasciotomy surgery, I was eager to move out of Hackensack University Medical Center — but up until my last days there, it wasn't quite clear where I should go. I wanted so badly to return home with my family, but I was far from healthy enough to do so. I was still dealing with the blood clot, my shoulder was still in delicate shape, and I still couldn't bear any weight on either leg. Unfortunately, our house wasn't properly set up to be wheelchair accessible, which meant that until I could, at the very least, bear enough weight on my legs to hobble around on crutches, I would have to stay at a rehabilitation facility.

Much as she had done when we were in New Mexico, Lynn used her skills as a negotiator to advocate for me, and we soon secured a room in the Kessler Institute for Rehabilitation in West Orange, New Jersey, which is one of the premiere physical rehabilitation hospitals in the nation.

On August 6, the day of my discharge from Hackensack, I was back in an ambulance. Although it was only a twenty-five-mile ride to West Orange, I still didn't enjoy it. I had come to hate riding in ambulances. Lying down, riding backward — the whole production, albeit necessary, was difficult.

But from the moment I arrived at Kessler, I sensed a good vibe. A sign on the wall read, "Motivating the Challenged, Challenging the Motivated." This sentiment really spoke to me. Clearly, they understood that, in order to heal, people needed both personal motivation and that little extra push to challenge them to keep at it.

My days at Kessler were much more structured than they had been at the other hospitals, and they emphasized encouraging patients to act independently. For example, breakfast was served in a dining room for those who were able to leave their rooms. I was determined to be one of the capable ones, and it was up to me to get in my wheelchair every morning and roll to breakfast. One thing I especially enjoyed about the breakfast at Kessler was that they had guava juice. I love guava juice. Even though it wasn't freshly squeezed (that would be too much to ask!), it was delicious, and it quickly became a small treat that I routinely looked forward to.

At breakfast, I sat with four other patients, all of whom were older than I was. It wasn't a talkative group, but when they did talk, they complained about their ailments.

I shared a room with three quadriplegics. Through the course of our conversations, I learned that two of these men had lost the ability to use their arms and legs in motorcycle accidents. I never learned what happened to the third, as he never spoke or even made eye contact with the rest of us. Being around these patients was a real wake-up call for me. For the first time, I truly appreciated *not* being the sickest guy in the wing. Although it was only a small shift, this realization helped build my sense of gratitude. I suddenly understood how much worse things could have turned out for me. I became very aware of how I spoke about my accident — to Lynn and to friends and colleagues who called on the phone. I realized that my roommates' journey to recovery was going to be very different than my own. Because of this, I didn't want to sound too upbeat about my progress, but on the other hand, I didn't want to complain about my situation and sound ungrateful, either. After all, I was lucky even to have the prospect of walking again. Occasionally, I would lie in bed at night and cry, listening to the rhythmic chimes of my roommates' medical equipment, imagining how things would have been different had something worse happened to me that morning in July.

In the daytime, I did my best to hold off these thoughts by keeping busy. That wasn't easy: even skimming the pages in a magazine like *People* or *US Weekly* would tire me out, and I couldn't focus on commercial television. Fortunately, my peloton members, like Derek McGinty — the same generous friend who had lent me his travel bike for my trip to New Mexico — sent me a bunch of DVDs to watch. Without those movies, I'm not sure how I would have made it through my waking hours. Eventually, as my energy and focus increased, I was able to read more sophisticated things than just magazines. Bill Sheldon, my company's CEO, gave me the novel *Memoirs of a Geisha* by Arthur Golden, which was the first book I was able to finish after my accident.

After a few days, I was transferred out of the room with the quadriplegics to a smaller room that I shared with a man named Phillippe. Phillippe was probably about twenty-five years older than me, and he was at Kessler for a broken tibia. He had been standing in the surf at the Jersey shore when an out-of-control boogie-boarder boogied right into him. Just like my own, his story was one of being in the wrong place at the wrong time. Phillippe was a bit of a comedy of errors. Not only did he get stung by a bee outside of the facility while trying to get some fresh air, but he also injured himself further when he tried to pick up something at his bedside and fell out of bed, breaking his arm. It was one thing after another for him, and luckily, he had an excellent sense of humor. He loved to watch the television show *Whose Line Is It Anyway?* Before long, he turned me on to it as well. Together, Phillippe and I would tune our separate televisions to the same channel and laugh in unison. To this day, whenever Lynn and I occasionally catch the show, it reminds me of Phillippe and how he brought a consistent dose of laughter to an environment that sometimes felt so heavy.

Twice a day, Lynn would make the trek to come visit me. In the mornings, she would come alone, bringing me a treat like a lemonade or a cookie, and sometimes she would even bring a whole meal that one of our friends had lovingly prepared. Although the meals at Kessler were the best to date, I was getting a little sick of hospital food. Whenever Lynn showed up carrying a Tupperware covered in foil, it was a magical moment. It amazed me that simple things like guava juice, lemonade, and a home-cooked meal suddenly were the things that I looked forward to the most.

In the afternoons, Lynn would frequently return for another visit with the girls. It was so great to see them regularly. I was able to hold Grady while I sat in my wheelchair, and although Elle was too big to do the same, I could still hug her, which I loved doing. Having Lynn and the girls with me, everyone together in the same room, made me feel that we were almost like a normal family again. Unfortunately, these visits would quickly drain me. It often wouldn't be more than half an hour before my head was bobbing and my eyelids were getting heavy. I felt badly that Lynn spent so much time in the car, driving to the facility and back, twice in one day. I wanted to make it worthwhile for her and the girls. I didn't want to be a dad who got tired from being around his children, who was so different than the dad they had remembered. But I was often so exhausted by their visits that regardless of what I wanted, I found I needed a nap immediately after.

In the morning I had physical therapy, which was intended to bring greater strength and range of motion to my arms and legs. On my first day, I wheeled my chair over to my physical therapist, Nicole. "Okay, we're going to start on the mat," she said energetically. "What's your strategy to get there?"

What's my strategy? I thought. I didn't need a strategy; it would be easy. I would just scoot myself from the wheelchair to the mat. Unfortunately, without the ability to bear any weight on my legs, this was easier said than done. I couldn't figure out how to do it. Nicole watched me as I struggled and worked up a sweat. Finally, she put me out of my misery, showing me how to get on the mat without hurting myself.

In the afternoon, I had occupational therapy to help me relearn the skills that I would need for daily life, like how to move independently around the house or how to be functional in the kitchen. In one session, I was given the task of baking chocolate chip cookies. This seemed absurd to me because, if I ever needed cookies, I could just buy them, or Lynn could make her famous oatmeal chocolate chip cookies, my favorite. However, my occupational therapist had other ideas on the matter. She felt that the range of motions required for baking cookies would help me with a variety of other useful activities, so I agreed to bake the cookies! It so happened that on that particular day, my boss's boss, Bill Sheldon, showed up for another visit. The fact that Bill came to visit me was significant. Given his position within our company, he had countless responsibilities. For him to give of his time to me is something I will never forget. It was an act of generosity that shaped me as a leader.

Possibly because the hospital didn't have all the ingredients, or possibly because I was distracted by Bill's company and left the cookies in the oven too long, the cookies turned out terribly. Most were burnt, and those that weren't scorched tasted just awful. Bill was a terrific sport, though, and insisted on eating one. Even though the cookies were a culinary failure, I did manage to do all the tasks required to bake them, and Bill didn't die from cookie poisoning, so I suppose it was a success after all.

At first, my progress in physical therapy was slow because the skin grafts on my left leg were still healing. Until they were better and the staples were removed, there was only so much that could be done. Luckily, after a week, all ninety-five staples were removed, and I got full clearance to do more intensive therapy on my left leg. Eventually, I was able to get on the exercise bike. This step was so important to me because, in my mind, getting back on the bike meant getting back to a level of normalcy. Yet I was frustrated that my left leg lacked significant range of motion. I had to take Percocet before my morning therapy session just to make it through the stretching of my leg. It was the kind of pain that left me sweaty and red in the face.

It wasn't even uncommon for me to cry a little through my therapy session. In truth, it wasn't just the pain that made me tear up. It was the anger, worry, and frustration that was constantly swirling around in my mind. As my body began its recovery, it became clearer and clearer just how many hurdles there were on the road to my recovery. I wanted my healing process to go faster, and I wanted it to be easier and less painful. I didn't want to be stuck in hospitals and rehab facilities, unable to care for my family or be of service to my company. I was growing more frustrated by having to show up for therapy, day after day, still unable to move my leg on the stationary bicycle, much less walk or bathe myself or do anything else that makes a person feel capable and independent. I felt I had lost my dignity.

I wanted this whole experience to be over, for my body and mind to be healed already, and I hated that I didn't have any control over how fast or effective my healing process was. I often found myself in a dark place.

⚙ WHEN I WOKE ON THE MORNING OF AUGUST 21, something was different. I can't really pinpoint how exactly, but something inside of me had shifted. I wheeled myself to breakfast, went to therapy, and got on the exercise bike as usual.

As Nicole, my physical therapist, attended to another patient, I took a moment to look around the room.

Because I had physical therapy at the same time every day, I had seen these same people day after day, and I had noted their struggles and their victories. Today, it was like I was seeing everything with new eyes. Around me were patients of all ages and with all sorts of injuries — from hip and knee replacements to full-body injuries like mine. This time as I looked around the room, I assessed who was making progress and who was stuck. For those who were making progress, what were they doing differently? What was the common thread between all of them?

What I observed astounded me. The thing that all these patients seemed to have in common was an optimistic mindset. They believed they were getting better, and this belief gave them the energy and momentum to keep moving forward. They had a different perspective. They not only celebrated when things went well, but they also took their setbacks in stride. It seemed to me these patients truly understood that healing was a question of mind over matter, that nothing could really change in the physical body until the mind had changed. A positive mindset wasn't necessarily a guarantee that they would improve, but I could see that it helped.

It felt like a giant lightbulb suddenly switched on in my mind. It was a moment of total consciousness. This was my shift, and nothing would be the same again.

I went back to my room and reflected on what I had seen, and I thought about my own attitude and mindset.

In that moment, I made a commitment to

myself that the next day would be a new

start. I would bring a new energy, drive,

and belief system to my recovery. . . .

In order to do this, I had to shift from the

perspective of a victim to that of a victor.

Even though I thought I was doing my best to stay positive, I had to admit, I wasn't showing up with a 100 percent positive attitude. I tried to imagine what others saw when they looked at me. Did I seem energetic? Optimistic? Was I giving my all? Or was I allowing emotions like anger, fear, and self-pity to drive my behavior?

When I saw myself from an outsider's perspective, it was sobering. Even though I was doing the best I could to put on my game face, trying to tack a positive narrative onto my story, in my heart, I didn't really believe it. In private, I was bitter and angry. I felt like a burden. I also realized that I probably wasn't fooling anybody. Taking a hard look at myself was illuminating, and the insight I gained from it was invaluable. In that moment, I made a commitment to myself that the next day would be a new start. I would bring a new energy, drive, and belief system to my recovery. If I was going to be the best husband, father, and person I could be, I had to stop thinking of "best" in comparison to other people or as an unattainable idea I had in my head. In order to do this, I had to shift from the perspective of a victim to that of a victor. This wasn't the life that I had planned for myself and my family, but it was an opportunity to be defined, not by what had happened to me, but by how I responded to it. The drive and desire to get better couldn't come from outside of myself: it had to come from the inside.

The next day I woke up early, and while most of the other patients were still asleep, I wheeled myself to a quiet section of the facility tucked away by some administrative offices. With none of the staff at work yet, this looked like the perfect secluded spot to get a positive mindset for the day. Remember, in 2001, the idea of mindfulness wasn't nearly as common as it is today. Not to mention that I didn't know a thing about meditation. But I wasn't going to let that stop me. I decided this was the day I would begin a new ritual. I put my favorite CD, Depeche Mode's *Violator,* in my Discman and pressed play. I played the whole album softly in my headphones as I focused on my breathing and the thoughts circulating in my head. I calmly took note of how I was feeling, what my focus was, and what I wanted to accomplish for the day. I discovered that the experience was calming, centering, and restorative. For the rest of that day, I found that I had a greater sense of clarity. I knew it was only one day, but already things seemed brighter and more hopeful. I decided this would be my new morning habit to set the day off right, with intention and focus.

The next day, I went to visit my orthopedic doctor. Unfortunately, the facility in West Orange didn't have an orthopedic specialist on staff, so I continued to see the doctor at Hackensack, the one I mentioned who lacked a desirable bedside manner. Every two weeks or so, I traveled in an ambulance to see him at his office. I hated going to that office. The waiting room felt like being in a New York subway car during rush hour. There were so many people I wondered if he was trying to see all his patients for the week in one day! When I finally saw him, his attention was all over the place. He would rush into the exam room, look briefly at an X-ray, give a prognosis, and then rush off to the next patient. He rarely gave me more than ten or fifteen minutes of his time.

Two days after I had my "shift," the news we received wasn't what we had wished for.

August 23, 2001
Subject: And the news is. . .

Unfortunately, not quite what we had hoped.

Hi everyone,
Today, Michael and I met with his orthopedic doctor in his office. . . . The doctor took X-rays of both Michael's legs and also his right shoulder.

The good news:

1. The scapula (right shoulder) fracture is totally healed. He has full range of motion and is already doing exercises and lifting weights with both arms.
2. The right leg continues to "lay good bone." The area around the fracture is all cloudy (on the X-ray), which means that the bone is growing like

crazy there and it's healing very well. There will be no need for a bone graft on that leg.

The not-as-good news:

1. Michael cannot begin weight-bearing exercises on either leg yet. He can start partial weight bearing on the right leg in two weeks. The doctor said he expects Michael to progress to full weight bearing "very rapidly." (I just love the precise time frames that the medical staff has been able to provide. . . .)

2. Michael cannot begin any weight bearing on his left leg for now. He returns to the doctor in four weeks — ironically enough, on his birthday (September 20) — for additional X-rays and will be evaluated then. I guess I don't have to tell you what he really wants for his birthday.

3. Michael will probably have to remain at Kessler for two to four more weeks, possibly more. Although Michael is very independent in his wheelchair and could consider coming home, our house is not really very wheelchair accessible and it would be logistically challenging. In addition, he would still need daily physical therapy sessions, which would mean continuing the forty-five-minute drive down to West Orange

and remaining for several hours while he has therapy. All of this is complicated, of course, by our young children.

Also, Michael has moved to another room. It's a double room and smaller than the (relatively) spacious four-person room he had before. At least he is not in his room as much as was necessary when he was in the regular hospital. If you send anything to him at Kessler, please do not even put a room number on it, in case he has to move again. They write down the room number when the mail arrives. He also has a new telephone number.

We are both, frankly, disappointed at the news from today's visit. We had hoped for at least partial weight bearing on one leg. To be told that it will be another two weeks before he can try is not what we had hoped to hear. The doctors and medical staff, however, continue to be very pleased with Michael's progress and are extremely optimistic. I think, in this case, our expectations were a bit high because we had not been given very much information and were therefore left to draw our own conclusions. We have to remind ourselves, sometimes, how thankful we are for the things that DIDN'T happen (spinal cord injury, head trauma, or internal organ damage). Being at Kessler, which specializes in spinal cord trauma, is actually very humbling in that regard.

We continue to be very grateful and touched by the outpouring of love and support that we have received. The steady stream of telephone calls, letters, T-shirts, and just *everything.*

Thank you all so much. Please keep those calls and the contact coming. We need it now, just as we did thirty-eight days ago when our lives were turned upside down.

Love, Lynn, Michael, Elle, and Grady

The news we received that morning at the orthopedic doctor's office was a blow to my newfound belief. It wasn't just that I was frustrated with the doctor's curt and abrupt manner, or that it felt like there was no other doctor who would take on my case. It was that the picture he painted — both verbally and nonverbally — of my future evoked a lifetime of limitations. That just wasn't acceptable to me anymore. I had shifted. I wanted more. If I couldn't have my old life back, I still wanted the best life possible, and a good life to me meant taking care of my family, having a meaningful role at my company, and of course, being active and riding again.

I felt stuck. I wanted to show what was possible with the right mindset, work ethic, and support system, but I worried that my doctor's pessimistic attitude wouldn't facilitate a positive outlook. I cried myself to sleep that night. I found myself thinking, *I would have been better off if they'd just cut my leg off.* Intellectually, of course, I knew that this wouldn't have been better, that my original hardware would always be better than a replacement part — but emotionally, I didn't feel that. My mind spiraled out of control as I dreamed of being in the Paralympics and winning all the cycling events with a prosthetic leg. That could have been my story, my great triumph, instead of the small triumph of bathing myself, which was still something I struggled with. I knew that these fantasies were coming from a place of ego, of wanting glory and praise, and from fighting against the hard work that was needed to heal my body.

It was a rough night, but I woke the next morning with a renewed sense of perseverance. The day was another opportunity to start fresh. I got out of bed, wheeled myself down the hall, put on my Depeche Mode CD, and focused on my breathing. It was time to tackle another day.

CHAPTER NINE

THE SHIFTING WORLD

Strength does not come from physical capacity. It comes from an indomitable will.

— GANDHI

Each day at Kessler began the same: reflection time, guava juice, and physical therapy. Depeche Mode was the soundtrack for my recovery, and the songs that played in my head on those days provided the inspiration to keep me positive and focused.

Other than the slow and steady progress on my leg, there was little difference from one day to the next. Until suddenly, everything was different.

The morning of September 11, 2001, began the same as any other day, but as I warmed up on the exercise bicycle, I overheard some of the therapists talking about how a small plane had crashed into the World Trade Center. From that first moment, my intuition told me that this was a far bigger deal than just an out-of-control Cessna taking a bad turn. I think we all remember where we were on that tragic day. There are only a few moments in my life that I can recall with complete vividness: the space shuttle *Challenger* explosion in 1986; both days that my daughters were born; my wedding day; July 11, the day of my accident; and now, September 11.

I called Lynn and told her to turn on the TV. She asked me which channel, and I told her, "Any channel."

After my therapy session, I wheeled myself back to my room. All the TVs in the facility, which were normally tuned to game shows, talk shows, and dramas, were now tuned to the news. You couldn't escape it even if you wanted to. Like everyone, I was glued to the television trying to understand what had happened and why. We were all in shock. It took a long time to fully comprehend the extent of the devastation.

Lynn and I had an overwhelming need for us to be together as a family. That afternoon, she put the girls in the car and drove to Kessler. As you might imagine, the traffic in the New York metro area on September 11 was pure chaos. Everyone was trying to get out of the city. From the car window Lynn could see the smoke rising up. A drive that normally took Lynn forty-five minutes took more than two hours, but I was so glad she decided to make the journey. Even though we felt emotionally drained, we needed all the love and support we could get that day. It was so important to spend time as a family right then, to be close to one another and try to process all that was happening.

The next afternoon, Lynn returned for a visit without the girls. As she wheeled me to the little gazebo on the grounds, I looked up at the sky and was struck by the absence of airplanes. Considering how close we were to Newark, LaGuardia, and JFK airports, the emptiness was eerie. As we sat soaking up the silent sunshine, we talked about the way the country had shifted so drastically in the past twenty-four hours.

In my opinion, September 12 was an opportunity for us as a nation. We had suffered a catastrophic setback, but the one thing I had learned in the past couple of months was that it's not what happens to you, but how you respond. For a moment, it seemed that we, as a nation, might respond well. There was a beautiful sense of togetherness in the air that reflected how truly interconnected we all are. What happens to one has an impact on all of us. The impact may not be direct, but we feel it. In the days after the towers collapsed, our tribe, our peloton, was strong. We were no longer divided as Democrats or Republicans, black or white, male or female. We threw off most of our labels.

I have to admit, in the days after September 11, it wasn't the national security issues that affected me the most. It was simply thinking about all the innocent people who had died that morning. The *New York Times* put out profiles of all the victims, and each day Lynn would read every one. For her it was an emotional process, but I found them hard to read. On television I saw the faces of men who looked just like me — young men in their thirties with young families. With every mention of, "He left behind a wife and their young daughters," I couldn't help but identify with many of the men killed that day. Knowing that these men were no longer able to be with their families or to provide for them just reminded me of how close I had come to being a statistic.

Stories were told of people who were not sitting at their desks in the World Trade Center that morning because of one simple thing: perhaps they took their child to their first day of kindergarten, or they went to work late due to the primary election that day in New York City. It reminded me again of how everyday choices, our moment-to-moment decisions, sometimes make the difference between life and death. What if I had decided to hit the snooze button on July 11? I never would have met that white SUV. On the flip side, had I left the hotel that morning only five or ten seconds earlier, I might have intersected with that SUV at a slightly different, and potentially more deadly, angle. If so, it's very possible that I might not have survived.

I lay in bed at night and thought about all the different ways that life could have gone on July 11. It was my own version of the movie *Sliding Doors*. I envisioned my obituary with the phrase "survived by his wife and two young daughters," and it filled me with such sadness.

During the day, it was easier to use these thoughts to fuel my recovery. For some reason, I had lived. It wasn't my time, and I had been given the opportunity to make a difference. This knowledge gave me the inspiration and motivation to keep pursing a positive mindset and to keep working at my recovery.

September 11, 2001
Subject: Michael Update

Hello Everyone,

As our nation digests the horrible, unspeakable acts of violence and terrorism committed today, somehow this update seems rather small and insignificant. In the last few days, however, a number of people have asked for some update on Michael, so I wanted to just check in with everyone.

Two weekends ago, Michael was granted a pass for weekend outings. Together, we learned how he can transfer from his wheelchair into the car, so now, usually once a week, I pick him up and we get out! We went to a movie two Saturdays ago and picked up some lunch, and this past weekend we went to one of our favorite stores and got lunch and fruit smoothies, and then went to the mall! It's nice for us to have some time away from Kessler and Michael enjoys being around people who are healthy and vibrant.

The four skins grafts on Michael's left leg have completely healed. He no longer has to wear bandages of any kind on that leg. Although right now the skin doesn't look like it did before, and he will have large scars, the leg looks good being out of all the bandages! The swelling is subsiding, too, which is not only more comfortable, but also aids with his flexibility and range of motion.

Yesterday was the first day for Michael to begin putting partial weight-bearing pressure on the right leg. Unfortunately, there seems to be a small breakdown in communication between the orthopedic doctor and the staff at Kessler, so the big changes we anticipated did not materialize, but he is making small changes in his therapy and in his routine. Now, for example, when he transfers from his wheelchair to bed or regular chair or anything, he can put his right foot down on the floor and apply pressure while he makes the transfer.

He no longer has to use the CPM machine, which gently and slowly bends his leg and then straightens it, on his right leg. He has achieved full flexibility on that leg! He still uses the machine on his left leg, in the evenings, but can devote the full four-hour time frame that he was previously dividing between the two legs to just his left leg. That motion helps reduce swelling, too.

We don't have an estimate yet from his doctors on his release date.

His spirits are good and we are focused on his release home. We eagerly await an estimated date for that. In the meantime, he has stayed "incarcerated" long enough to catch the Vuelta a Espana (the Tour of Spain — it's a major cycling event, for the noninitiated among us), and at least as long as he's bed-bound, he can catch a lot more of it at Kessler than he would at home!

The rest of the family is holding up well. Elle, almost four years old, starts her first day of preschool tomorrow. She's very excited about that. Grady is nearly eleven months old, and cruising like crazy. She is definitely going to give Daddy a run for his money in the Race to Walk First. I am very busy, as you might imagine, but I'm visiting Michael almost every day and trying to keep things at home on an even keel. It's not always easy, especially when you're an accident-prone person like myself. Just in the past week, I had to make a trip to the ER (I closed the hatchback door of my car on my face) and get three stitches on the bridge of my nose. Then, I had an allergic reaction to the medicine the doctor used on the stitches and that required an emergency visit to the dermatologist to have it treated! Ah, when it rains it pours. We decided to write this whole summer off.

Today's tragic events in New York, Washington, DC, Pennsylvania, and elsewhere remind us that our lives and our health are precious. We continue to be grateful for our own health as well as for your continued calls, notes, thoughts, emails, packages and well-wishes. Thank you very much.

Finally, for those of you who considered blood donation after our initial post-accident pleas, but have not yet found or made the time, I hope you will put it on the top of your list now. I'm going tomorrow.

Love, Lynn

A few days before September 11, I was granted clearance to leave Kessler on a day pass. Straightaway, Lynn and I made plans for our first date since the accident: dinner and a movie.

We went to a small Italian restaurant in West Orange, New Jersey. It was great to be out of the hospital and in a different environment for a change. It wasn't exactly familiar territory for me to visit a restaurant in a wheelchair, but it was a start, a small return to normal.

The movie we saw that night was *Serendipity* with John Cusack and Kate Beckinsale. I loved it. The sentiment of the movie — that a small, seemingly random moment can have a profound impact on your life — wasn't lost on me. It was a great date night, one of our best.

A few days later I got a second pass, and Lynn and I decided to go to the Garden State Plaza in Paramus. As we entered the parking lot, I saw a big white Ford SUV coming our way. I tensed up as shivers ran down my spine.

My reaction was a clear sign I still had a long road to travel before I was fully recovered.

Navigating between the car and the mall proved difficult. There were cracks in the pavement and breaks in the sidewalk. In many spots, there was no ramp or even access to and from the sidewalk. Whenever I left Kessler, I became aware of all the minor obstacles, which I once easily walked right over, that for a wheelchair were huge and unwieldy. Nothing was ever easy — like parking and leaving enough room to get out of the car or needing the restaurant waitstaff to rearrange the tables for me. Everyone did their best to be helpful, but it always felt like a production. I didn't want to make a scene or be a burden. I just wanted to be a normal guy who could go out on a date with his wife. Today, whenever I see someone in a wheelchair, I appreciate what they navigate on a daily basis.

Once inside the mall, things were easier. I could zip along the shiny marble floors and pick up some speed down the ramps. Although I was probably only going about five miles an hour, it felt fast and reminded me of riding a bicycle. It felt good to move quickly on two wheels again.

Still, I quickly became self-conscious about being a person in a wheelchair. In the past, I would be in and out of the mall without noticing much about the people around me. I have always been a focused buyer versus the kind of person who hangs out at the mall. From my wheelchair, I took note of how many people glanced our way. I interpreted their glances as pity. I could hear what I imagined was going through their heads: *Who's that guy? What happened to him? What's with all his cuts and scars?* The movie in my head was still a drama, and I was the main act.

I realize now that those people at the mall probably weren't paying very much attention to me. They had enough going on in their own lives to not even notice me. Or if they were looking at me, it's just as plausible that their looks were intended to convey sympathy or motivation. I chose to perceive a negative emotion, and this choice planted a seed of further self-consciousness in me. There's a saying I like to use now, whenever I'm feeling self-conscious: "You'll be less worried about what people think about you when you realize that they don't spend a lot of time thinking about you." It helps me remember that most people are too busy thinking about themselves and their own lives to even notice you. In a small way, this understanding has been extremely liberating.

ON SEPTEMBER 20, I TURNED THIRTY-FOUR. I HAD been looking forward to this day for a number of reasons, not least of all because I had another appointment with my orthopedic doctor. My biggest birthday wish was to get a thumbs-up to start putting full weight on both legs. That morning, after I scored a second glass of guava juice as an early birthday gift, I had a great physical therapy session. We prepared for my appointment later that day with a warm-up on the bike followed by strength and flexibility exercises.

That afternoon, I was determined not to let my personal feelings about the doctor get in the way of anything. I was determined to make today different. To my delight, the doctor granted that birthday wish! I was so relieved and excited that I wanted to share the news immediately. Lynn called Kessler and told my therapists the good word, and when we returned that afternoon, we found the whole team waiting for us. Most of them should have left for the day, but they wanted to stay to celebrate this important milestone with us, and I was eager to begin the process of walking again.

I went straight to the physical therapy gym, and I rolled my wheelchair beside the parallel bars. Nicole asked me her trademark question: "What's your strategy?" I didn't have an answer; I had no plan. I just knew I wanted to walk again. I got up slowly, awkwardly, and cautiously. Looking down the length of the parallel bars, I was intimidated. They were probably only about twelve feet long, but it looked like a mile. Pushing against the parallel bars with my arms to help support my weight, I propped myself up, getting a little dizzy in the process. For the first time in nine weeks, I was upright. I took my first step and then a second. I had to stop and rest. It was harder than I imagined and took so much upper body strength. After a little break, I managed to make it across and back. As I sat back down in my chair, the sweat dripped down my forehead. Those were some of the toughest steps I had ever taken in my life, but I was pumped.

I did three more reps that afternoon, and by the end, it felt like I had ridden my bike a hundred miles! I was exhausted. It was an emotionally and physically draining experience, but I felt good about entering a new phase of my recovery.

Along with my shift in mindset, this moment was one of the most significant turning points in my journey back to health. The next day we started talking about when I could leave Kessler. It wouldn't be long now.

September 20, 2001
Subject: He Walks!!

Hello everyone,
Today Michael had the long-anticipated doctor's appointment and received wonderful news: he has permission to bear his full weight on his right leg and to go to partial weight bearing on the left leg! We went back to Kessler, and he was able to stand up and walk for the first time in over ten weeks using the parallel bars and the therapy guys to assist him. The moment brought tears to our eyes as well as those of his therapists. We're

all so thrilled. It was the best birthday present he could have received.

AND what's more: he's coming home on the twenty-eighth! He will continue his physical therapy at Kessler, five times a week. We hope that he will be on crutches full-time by then, but even if he is in a wheelchair, at least he will be home with the family. We are so happy about that.

He continues to ride the recumbent bike in his therapy sessions and is now doing forty minutes each day (more if he can get away with it!) and getting his cardiovascular system back in shape. His resting heart rate is already down in the fifties, even closer to his ridiculously low pre-accident rate.

His skin grafts have completely healed, and he no longer has any bandages on his body. He is using the CPM machine on one leg still, to help achieve greater range of motion. The other leg has recovered almost complete range of motion so the machine no longer helps him — he can do as much or more without it.

As Michael said on his way to therapy today, "Finally, I can see the light at the end of the tunnel." It seems as though this difficult time is finally winding down. We are grateful for, among other things, your support, friendship, love, assistance, grocery and bagel runs, prayers, and well-wishes. As we continue to struggle with emotions resulting from last week's national tragedy, we are thankful to be together as a family and to be part of the larger community that includes all of you.

Thank you.

In peace, Lynn

I wish I could tell you that I was radically changed from that moment on. But the truth was, my shift was slow, and the progress wasn't always apparent. My transformation happened incrementally, with more than a few instances of sliding backward. But the ability to walk was a clear indication of progress. Perhaps it took a tangible, physical result to really show me that the hard work I had been doing was paying off and that change was possible.

I started to go to physical therapy early every morning, filled with a strong desire to work. I wanted to get as much time on the bicycle as possible. It wasn't always easy, but I just wanted to move. Instead of feeling defeated when I was exhausted after therapy, I started to see it as a good thing because it meant I was putting in all my effort. I created a mantra: "Make tomorrow better than today." It provided focus and hope as I repeated this to myself during those days. It was all about being responsible for improving my future.

Little by little, my strength and range of motion increased. Over time, my energy increased as well. I had more energy for Lynn and the kids. Things that once seemed frustrating or defeating didn't seem so impossible anymore. The dark cloud over my head started to clear. When people told me, "You're so lucky," it no longer bugged me. Instead of letting the possibility of how bad it could have been terrify me, this sentiment finally started to truly inspire me. That small understanding opened the door a crack to a greater realization and acceptance of what had happened to me.

Less than two weeks after my birthday and those monumental first steps, it was time for me to go home.

CHAPTER TEN

RETURN TO LIFE

*How can you know
what you are capable
of if you don't embrace
the unknown?*

— ESMERALDA SANTIAGO

was so excited to be back in my own home, to sleep in my own bed, to be around my family again, and to get back to work. Finally, on September 28, I returned home, and my life could return to normal. Well, at least a new normal.

In the following few years, people often asked me, "Michael, are you back to normal yet?" Each time, this question gave me pause. Back then, I didn't know how to define normal or when I might feel normal again. I suppose in many ways I was searching for a new normal. I was looking to make tomorrow better than today, making improvements, and leveling up. Returning home was certainly a step in the right direction, but I wasn't even sure I could take a shower or navigate the steps to the second floor in my own home.

Nevertheless, it was a relief to see our house come into view as we pulled down our little street and into the driveway. Whenever we went away for vacation, I was always happy to return home, and this time it felt especially good. Using my crutches for support, I navigated out of the car to the front door. It wasn't easy. While I could put full weight on both of my legs, it wasn't like I could go for a power walk or anything like that. I was still suffering from limited dorsiflexion, a lack of balance, and peroneal nerve damage in my left foot. This meant that sometimes pain like an electric shock would shoot up my left leg, seemingly out of nowhere. Walking took a great amount of focus, as I had to make sure my left toes would flex enough to lift over rugs or uneven surfaces.

It wasn't long before I thought about going back to work. This was about more than just getting back to a familiar routine: after devoting all my time and energy to recovery, I was eager to finally think about something else. Besides, I believed in the mission of the company, and I wanted to be able to contribute to their work while feeling as if I was providing for my family.

I reached out to my company and told them I wanted to return. They were excited to hear from me, and we worked out a schedule where I could go to work three days a week and then go to physical therapy on the other days.

On October 10, my first day back, I traveled to our sales meeting in East Rutherford, New Jersey. I was nervous. I wondered how I would be greeted. Was I still needed? Was I still wanted? Compounding my jitters, I was also running late — something that I detest — having underestimated how long it would take me to shower, shave, and dress professionally. When I arrived, the meeting had already started, so I did my best to slide discreetly into the back of the room, but a few colleagues saw me and gave me warm smiles and thumbs up. Then, at the first opportunity for a break, the entire meeting greeted me with a warm round of applause. Even though this attention was a little embarrassing, I was glad my worries had been unfounded.

The very next week we had a meeting for the entire sales force. It would be our first meeting since June, which for me felt like a lifetime ago. The meeting was being held at the nearby Sheraton in East Rutherford, and I had been asked to present on stage. While the request was flattering, I had been away from the company for a few months. Since our last meeting in June, the whole world had changed, and everyone was still in the process of coming to grips with 9/11. For many of our colleagues flying in from other parts of the country, this would be both their first flight and their first visit to the New York area since the tragedy.

The meeting started off well, if predictably, with the usual information, but the tone changed abruptly when we watched a video message sent by our Tokyo-based chairman. He spoke sympathetically about the tragic events of September 11. Although his remarks were thoughtful, caring, and well-intentioned, he nevertheless brought our attention back to the very thing that everyone was working so hard not to focus on. You could feel the energy of the ballroom shift. As people wiped tears from their eyes, I thought to myself, "This is going to be a tough act to follow." My team decided it would be best to take an impromptu break to allow people to go to the bathroom, get a drink of water, and refocus.

After the break, I gathered up all my energy to walk out on stage. I didn't want to use my crutches — that wasn't the visual message I was trying to send. Conveniently, the meeting had a baseball theme, so I limped out slowly but steadily, supporting my weight on a baseball bat. As soon as I stepped into the spotlight, the entire room rose in a standing ovation. The whole team — both people whom I had known for years and people I had just met, who would never know me as I was before July 11 — stood in rousing applause. It was a powerful moment.

I got choked up and only just managed to hold back the blubbering. It was good to be back.

ON MY DAYS OFF, I RETURNED TO KESSLER TO meet with my new physical therapist, Cindy. I instantly liked her. She was totally direct, no-nonsense, and wanted to get going immediately. In addition to building strength and stamina, I had to increase the flexibility of my left leg. When riding the stationary bicycle, my pedal stroke was choppy at best. It looked more like a trapezoid than a beautiful circle. I couldn't flex my knee more than 80 degrees, so I would cheat by shifting my hips or lifting my butt, but this wasn't ergonomically sound or effective. I would need at least 95 to 100 degrees of flexibility if I ever hoped to really ride a bicycle again. On the other end, I couldn't quite extend it either. At six o'clock on the pedal stroke, my leg seemed too short, but at twelve o'clock it was too long. This created a strange predicament.

Cindy was determined to get that leg moving. She insisted I premedicate with Percocet before I arrived at physical therapy. Though I still wasn't thrilled about having to take painkillers, I'm glad she insisted! To move my leg, I would lie down on the mat on my stomach, while a second physical therapist would pin me down like we were in a wrestling match. Then Cindy would use her entire body weight to push my leg up into a flexed position while a third physical therapist measured the degree of flexibility. I would lie there, holding my breath, sweating, and gripping the mat for dear life. It was so painful — and I'm sure, quite a spectacle!

I admired Cindy's determination, but after three months, even she had to admit that the leg just wasn't budging. We couldn't get the left leg's flexion past 85 degrees. In its eagerness to heal, my body had laid down a massive amount of new bone and scar tissue. Now this tissue was keeping my knee from reaching its full flexibility.

I sank into a funk again. Even though several weeks ago I had realized I needed to shift my mindset if I wanted to be the father, husband, and person that I wanted to be, I now realized that awareness was one thing, but acceptance is another. I felt like I had taken two steps forward, and now, begrudgingly, I had to take a step back. I did my best to keep a positive demeanor, saying, "What doesn't break you makes you stronger." But deep down, I wondered if all of this was breaking me. The fear that I would never get back on my bike weighed heavily on me. At Kessler, I had made a commitment to myself that I wouldn't be defined by my accident but by how I responded to it. I wanted to embody the qualities I admired, like grit and determination. Until I was back on the bike, I knew I hadn't reached my goal.

It became clear to my physical therapists and to me that I would need yet another surgery.

But who would do it? There was no way that I was going to let my current orthopedic surgeon anywhere near me with sharp objects. I considered going back to New Mexico, where Dr. Schenck had offered to work with me, but ultimately, Lynn and I decided this would be too complicated. In the end, Dr. Schenck gave me the name of another surgeon who was a bit closer to home. Dr. Thomas Wickiewicz was a surgeon at the Hospital for Special Surgery in New York City. He was very highly regarded and had an impressive list of credentials, which made him an ideal choice for my surgery — but first, we had to convince him to take me on as a patient.

When I first reached out to Dr. Wickie — as I would come to call him affectionately — I couldn't get an appointment. As a trauma patient, my case was complicated and surrounded by lots of unspoken concerns. Luckily, Dr. Schenck wrote a compelling letter to his colleague asking him to consider seeing me, and Dr. Wickiewicz agreed.

On February 5, 2002, I went into New York City to meet with this prestigious surgeon. He examined my case and sat me down for a very frank conversation. He told me that, given the magnitude of my trauma, I had made a remarkable recovery. I was lucky that I could walk and have the function that I had. He warned me that the surgery would be complicated, and yet he wouldn't really know what he was dealing with until he opened my knee up. Orthopedic surgery is like carpentry. It's precise, but it requires a certain degree of forcefulness. If he accidentally cut the bypass graft, I could be looking at an above-the-knee amputation. He looked at me frankly and asked, "How badly do you really want to ride your bike?"

I gave his question some thought. When I reflected back on my life, I had the sneaking feeling that I hadn't really tapped into my full potential. Schoolwork, sports, relationships — I rarely gave it a hundred percent. I always told myself I was giving it my all, but in reality, too frequently I coasted. This isn't necessarily a bad thing. Sometimes it feels safer to coast. It can feel less risky. And even at this steady, easy pace, I had still gotten pretty far in life — I had a great marriage, two wonderful daughters, a good career, and many close friends. But ever since my accident, I had the feeling that I didn't want to be stuck in this comfort zone anymore. On a bicycle, when you coast, you stop building momentum, and eventually you get left behind. I no longer wanted to coast. I wanted to keep pedaling.

I looked back at Dr. Wickie. "I want this pretty badly," I said candidly.

In preparation for the surgery, I had a magnetic resonance angiogram (MRA) in March. The results suggested I had a pseudoaneurysm, or false aneurysm, measuring 12.5 centimeters off the popliteal artery, which stretches across the back of the knee and leg. A pseudoaneurysm is a collection of blood that forms because of a leaking hole in the artery and is relatively common with arterial trauma. Although it was doubtful, I couldn't help but wonder if this was part of the reason I couldn't get my left leg to flex normally. Unfortunately, this development added another layer of complexity to the surgery. Once again, I was given the opportunity to opt out of the operation, but I was determined to go through with it. For added safety, Dr. Wickie asked an acclaimed vascular surgeon, Dr. Gary Fantini, to assist in the surgery. With two experts at the top of their field on the surgical team, I felt even more confident in my choice.

On May 15, a day after our eighth wedding anniversary, Lynn and I arrived at the hospital. It was a beautiful Wednesday morning, and as we pulled into the parking lot at seven in the morning, Dr. Wickiewicz was right behind us. We were early, of course, but I was eager to check in, get prepped, and get on the operating table. After a surgery premeeting with Dr. Wickiewicz, a nurse wheeled me into the operating room. I greeted the anesthesiologist, who asked me to count backward from ten. I was fast asleep before I got to the number four.

The surgery was a great success. Not only was the pseudoaneurysm smaller than the MRA had suggested, but the surgical team was able to create 120 degrees of flexion on the left leg — more than enough to start riding my bicycle again. The surgery also gave Dr. Wickiewicz a clear, inside view of my injuries. Back in recovery, I joyfully made a deal with Dr. Wickie that I wouldn't be back for a knee replacement until long after he had retired. If I ever needed that, it would be a very complicated surgery.

With my fourth surgery complete, it was time to get back to rehab. Although the operation had been successful, it still remained to be seen whether the leg could maintain that flexibility. I returned to Kessler to work with a new physical therapist, Laura Fucci (Cindy was now on maternity leave). I liked Laura right away. A former weight lifter and bodybuilder and a current triathlete, Laura had all the drive and determination that was so crucial for this stage of my recovery. She immediately pushed me harder than any other therapist I had seen so far. In order to regain the strength in my legs and core, Laura had me do what she called "thirteen by thirteen" squats. The goal was to do thirteen reps of weighted squats on a down and up count of three, then rest for forty-two seconds, and then do it again, eventually doing thirteen sets — hence the name. The goal is to move slowly and carefully. While the first set doesn't seem challenging, by the sixth or seventh, you can really feel the burn. Thirteen by thirteen became a rehab staple for me, and I still do them to this day.

The other focus of physical therapy was to increase my flexibility. The goal was to have the scar tissue grow around the range of motion, rather than limit it. Laura would have me lie on my belly on a table, holding my breath while she cranked on my leg, putting all her body weight up against it, trying to make it move. Laura was the strongest physical therapist I had had to date. That was good for getting deeper into the tissue, but it also meant going deep into the pain cave. I would hold my breath and curse at Laura, but she would just laugh. In the end, I realized that you can't escape pain, but suffering is optional. The pain was temporary, and we made real progress on my leg. During these sessions, I found myself repeating my little mantra: "Make tomorrow better than today. Make tomorrow better than today." I knew that the work I put in today would make tomorrow better. It might only be a single degree of improvement in my range of motion, but it was a degree better, nevertheless.

Slowly, session by session, I grew stronger and more flexible. When I had my first session with Laura, I could

I knew that the work I put in today

would make tomorrow better. It might

only be a single degree of improvement

in my range of motion, but it was

a degree better, nevertheless.

get to about 96 degrees of flexibility without a warm-up. After six weeks, we had achieved between 115 and 120 degrees with a warm-up and Laura pushing on my leg. Gaining those 24 degrees required some of the hardest work I have ever done in my whole life, but the accomplishment also illustrated what I was capable of. I was starting to realize that being the greatest doesn't come from easy, it comes from hard.

Laura could see I was thriving on the challenges she was throwing me. She told me later that, as she did with every patient, she had to assess the best way to motivate me. "I knew you were an accomplished cyclist, and you guys are tough cookies. If you can ride in a pack like they do and crash like they do and go through the brutal training that they do to get to that level of cycling, I figured, well, this guy can take it." She could also see how much getting back on the bike mattered to me. "If you define yourself by your successes and your passions, then you're told you can't do it anymore, it's a wound to the psyche. I didn't see any reason why you couldn't get back riding. That was the number-one goal: to get you back on the bike."

I loved going to therapy. It was a nice, social environment, and I could make incremental progress with the positive encouragement of my physical therapists. In truth, although it was painful, it felt comfortable and good to be doing the work. I was cool with it — maybe a little too cool. In fact, I preferred it to moving to the next step: getting back on the bike, which, as I got closer to it, made me increasingly anxious. I delayed that ultimate goal because, I had to admit, I was scared. Yes, I was afraid of riding in traffic, but, deep down, I knew I could handle that. I was more afraid of learning how much further I still had to go.

Finally, Laura gave me an ultimatum: until I got back on the bicycle, I couldn't come back to rehab. I wasn't happy about this, but deep down, I knew she was right. I knew that if I didn't push myself outside of my comfort zone, I would be settling for less than my best. Getting on the bike meant facing the distance between where I was currently and where I still wanted to go.

On Saturday, August 11, almost a month past the one-year anniversary of my accident, Lynn, Elle, Grady, and I piled in our minivan and drove to an industrial park in Rockleigh, New Jersey, that was used for our local Thursday night criterium race. A criterium, or crit, is a race that consists of multiple laps of a loop, usually ½–1½ miles. A full criterium race may last 45 to 75 minutes. In this case, it was a perfectly flat, one-mile loop without any traffic.

I had two bicycles at the time: my old Serotta and a titanium bicycle from Titus purchased before my accident. After my college graduation, I got into running and did the Marine Corp and Boston marathons. Then I started competing in duathlons as a way of combining running and cycling. I bought the Titus as a motivator to get me back into full-time cycling. With its custom Tour de France paint scheme, it seemed to represent the greatness I hoped to find in myself. The front of the bicycle was "maillot jaune" yellow, the color representing the leader of the Tour, the so-called "yellow jersey." The middle of the bicycle was painted with red polka dots. The best climber of the Tour de France (the King of the Mountains) wears a jersey with this pattern. And the back of the bike was green, which is the color of the jersey worn by the best sprinter of the Tour. The Tour de France is the pinnacle aspiration for cyclists. This was the perfect bike for my first ride.

I lifted my bike off the rack, checked that it was set up correctly, and I climbed on. As I started to pedal forward slowly, I could feel the bike shake beneath me. My balance was off, and the difference in length between my two legs made my pedal stroke choppy. I kept pedaling, finding pleasure in the movement.

Lynn and the girls watched me get going, and then as we'd planned, they gave me some alone time. I continued to pedal, but after about five or six laps, I started to get bored with the safe (from cars but not potholes) little one-mile loop around some nondescript redbrick buildings. Although I had heard about the Thursday night crit races since we moved to New Jersey in 1998, I never had the chance to do them because of the demands of my career and parenthood. This was my first time on the course and given my pace, around 11 to 12 miles per hour, the scenery

*Above: On August 11, 2002, Elle (then four years old)
watches me get ready for my first ride since my last bad day.*

was uninspiring. I could only assume that if I were racing this loop, at a typical race pace of 24 to 26 miles per hour, I would be filled with adrenaline. But today I wasn't racing.

Even though my pedaling stroke felt far from smooth given my shorter left leg and lack of muscle symmetry, I decided to make a bold move to grab a little adrenaline and change the scenery. I broke away from the industrial park and ventured out onto Piermont Road.

Piermont Road was a common segment in my training rides as I returned to cycling, as it connected Tenafly with Rockland County, New York. It was also often used by other cyclists in the area. The local "Rocket Ride" can be found flying down it every Sunday morning at speeds sometimes hitting 30 plus miles per hour. I started doing this ride to prepare for my return to racing, but I would usually get dropped on the climbs at the end of the ride. To this day, it's the best ride in the area to test your racing fitness.

Piermont Road is flat and has light traffic, at least by New Jersey standards. I thought I could ride a few miles north to Piermont, New York, and turn around before Lynn and the girls returned to the industrial park. I believed my plan was perfect, and I could surprise them with my accomplishment.

Within a minute of making this decision, however, I could hear a vehicle approaching from behind. I quickly glanced over my shoulder and saw a speeding SUV coming right behind me. I couldn't believe it! Of all the vehicles in the world, this was the first one to come my way. The universe works in mysterious ways. Given my pace, which was still just about 12 miles per hour, I knew the SUV would be on me in a matter of seconds. I moved as close to the right side of the road as possible and kept pedaling. I could feel my breathing get shallower and shallower as my grip on the handlebars grew tighter and tighter. As the SUV was getting closer, I could feel its vibration on the road and hear the engine humming along. When it was only about twenty-five feet or so behind me, I closed my eyes, held my breath, and hoped for the best. Then, in a blink, it passed. I opened my eyes and saw the rear of the SUV travel off into the distance. I exhaled and softened my grip on my handlebars. A huge smile spread across my face. I did it! It was a true "Go-Me" moment.

I had passed my biggest milestone to date. I knew then I could handle riding on the road and in traffic. If I was unfortunate enough to have something happen to me again while bicycling on the road, then it was just my time. I couldn't live life curled up on the couch, too afraid to truly live.

CHAPTER ELEVEN

JUST KEEP PEDALING

*The energy of the mind
is the essence of life.*

— ARISTOTLE

n the years that followed, I experienced many more shifts; some were small and incremental, and others were more abrupt and significant. Although the "normal" I had once hoped for never quite returned, I came to realize that even if I hadn't had my accident, my life would still have kept changing. Only now, every aspect of my life was informed by one moment in time and all that followed. Who knows who I would have become had I never come in contact with that SUV? Having lived through this experience, I found that I shifted in ways that I never would have imagined.

I certainly haven't always felt this way, but from my current vantage point, more than fifteen years later, I can safely say that I'm pleased this is the road that life took me down. It's immensely gratifying to be able to look back now to see how far I've come.

After my accident, things at work changed almost immediately. I was asked to step into a new role as director of sales operations. I wasn't immediately excited about this role. Back in the 1970s, when Xerox pioneered the whole area of sales operations, group leader J. Patrick Kelly described it as "all the nasty number things that you don't want to do but need to do to make a great sales force." At my company, I had heard the leaders of the department refer to it as the "land of misfit toys" because it seemed made up of so many disconnected parts. In the end, I changed my perspective: I realized I was being entrusted with the task of making all those separate pieces fit together. Not only that, the position demanded less travel and allowed me to spend more time at home. Then, my team's success at turning the department around made me realize that my abilities were much broader than I imagined. I wasn't just a marketer and I wasn't just a sales guy. My skills weren't specific to my department; they were the skills of grit, motivation, and adaptability. Most importantly, I realized that my most valuable skill was my talent for getting people to work together. Once I understood this, I felt a new sense of direction, and I was able to move into a series of leadership positions, working across both sales and marketing.

Sometimes it's easier for others to see the changes in you than it is for you to see them in yourself. Darren Heath, a colleague, had known me before the accident, and afterward he worked directly for me. Darren said he had always considered me a courageous kind of person, but when I returned after the accident, I seemed totally without fear and with a new sense of purpose. "You seemed to step up more," he said. "You became more energetic about being that person that people looked to. Everyone knew what you had been through, and they were inspired by that."

I returned to cycling and was even more passionate and committed than before. It was humbling to revisit my old routes and see how my body had changed in the time away, but I was determined to build up my skills again. After a period of solid training, I was ready to take part in a ride from Ground Zero in New York City all the way to Washington, DC, in summer 2003. That three-day, three-hundred-mile ride was very meaningful for me: it traveled from a place with such political and cultural importance to a place with such personal associations — after all, Washington was where Lynn and I first met years before. I rode a few miles with a childhood cycling hero, Nelson Vails (silver medalist at the 1984 Olympic Games), as well as disabled cyclists whose perseverance was inspiring. Near the finish line, I admit I got a little choked up. It was such a sense of personal accomplishment, and I felt immense gratitude for all those who had helped me along the way.

I followed this up with a series of rides, each one increasing my strength and courage to return to racing. Then, on July 10, 2008, I finally pinned a number to my jersey again and took my place with the racing peloton.

My first race was on the same course I had ridden that first day back on the bicycle in 2002. This time, however, I wasn't afraid of any oncoming SUVs because I knew that riding in a peloton was actually safer than riding on the road, and it therefore made me confident. I was reminded of what it is that makes moving forward with a

Above: Standing on the Capitol Building Lawn in Washington, DC, with Elle (5), Grady (2) and bear, at the end of my three-hundred-mile charity ride from Ground Zero in New York on my Tour de France bike.

pack such a special sensation. The rush that comes from riding shoulder-to-shoulder with your fellow cyclists is a powerful motivator.

Even as my strength and stamina increased, I had more than a few setbacks. From a bone chip popping out of my knee to the removal of a femur rod and screws (from the initial trauma surgery), I had a bunch of reasons to go under the knife again. Sometimes these surgeries meant I had to return to the hospital for days, or even weeks, and they always seemed to come at a time when things were changing at work. Sometimes these changes were for the better; sometimes they were difficult. However, change always creates stress, even if it's for the best. By this point, though, the process of undergoing surgery had become somewhat routine. I approached it in a more businesslike way because I knew I would recover.

For almost a decade, I did the best I could to make life feel as stable and secure as possible. I worked at my job, kept myself active and strong on the bicycle, and spent time with my family, watching my daughters grow up. It seemed like my routine, my family, and my healing were at last stable, maybe even back to "normal." Then, in 2008, soon after I was promoted to vice president of sales, our company prepared for two game-changing events. Two of our major drugs were becoming available in generic form, which put a great deal of financial pressure on the company. From 2010 to 2014, my team had to be downsized by

60 percent. As a leader, it was my responsibility to let people go. I had to let my friends go — people I had worked with, whose families I knew. It pained me, although I tried not to show it, to have to dismantle my team, to take something apart that we had all worked so hard to build. Nevertheless, it was part of my job.

In 2014, the company went through even more changes, and they asked me to take on another role in the company. By this point, the stress of the numerous downsizings had taken a toll on me; in general, I was exhausted and unhappy. My daughters were now teenagers, and I didn't want my girls to see me like that. I wanted to be able to say to them, "Listen, regardless of your age, you can always reinvent yourself. You can always change your story." I knew I had to make a change.

I thought back on the people and moments in my career that had been the most impactful, and my mind immediately went to David Kolb. He was the business coach whose name I had repeated to Lynn in my drug-induced haze in the days after my accident. I enjoyed his calm demeanor and his refreshing perspective, and I admired his ability to find solutions that helped everyone feel that they had won. He was the first business coach I had ever met, back at a time when I didn't even know that was a career option. More than anyone I had met in all my years in business, David Kolb was the person whose footsteps I most wanted to follow.

I thought back to a particular conversation I had had while on the ride from Ground Zero to Washington, DC. I was pedaling beside a young woman, telling her about my accident and my long road to recovery to return to the saddle. As we pedaled, she said to me in between breaths, "You should be a coach." She meant a cycling coach, but the reason wasn't because I was the fastest or the strongest cyclist in the ride. She said she suggested it because hearing me telling my story inspired her.

After my accident, many health care professionals told me that a full recovery wouldn't be possible, but even when I was laid up in the hospital, I imagined myself getting back on the bike. Even when I was told that I might have to live with extreme limitations, I envisioned myself back at work. It wasn't always easy, and I have to admit I didn't always accept my setbacks gracefully. I often disappointed myself, feeling like I wasn't keeping a positive attitude or that I was losing sight of my goal. But I always kept trying, and over time, I came to realize that it matters far more that you get back on the bike than that you have fallen.

At the time, I was surprised and flattered when my fellow cyclist made this suggestion to me, and somewhere in the back of my mind, it validated something I had been considering since my time in the hospital. Now, as I found myself contemplating whether to accept an executive role in the company or to pursue a different professional avenue,

I was pedaling beside a young woman, telling her about my accident and my long road to recovery . . . she said to me in between breaths, "You should be a coach." . . . Hearing me telling my story inspired her.

that conversation, along with the thought of David Kolb, floated into my mind.

I believe that the universe is always trying to tell us something. People and events come and go in our lives. There's always a reason, but it's up to us to have the awareness to figure out what it is.

Ultimately, I decided to leave my company and start my own executive- and team-coaching business. Many of my coworkers were surprised when I left. I told my team I was retiring, but I wasn't really retiring. I wasn't quitting; I was being pulled toward something greater. To the people who knew me well, this was the move that fitted best. As my buddy and colleague Darren said to me afterward, "You could have gone and parlayed your experience into another role, where you could have made a lot of money. But when you told me what you were going to do, I thought, *Yeah, that sounds like Michael. That makes sense.*"

From my perspective, all the years since my accident had been a journey leading right to this point. I came to consider July 11, 2001, as my "last bad day" because my accident, and all that happened after, made me conscious of the impact I wanted to make on the world. Since that morning in 2001, I had learned so much. It was time to begin a new chapter in the journey, one in which I helped other people learn from my experience.

I named my coaching business Peloton, after the pack of cyclists in a bicycle race. A peloton is my type of tribe.

I wanted to help people understand that we are faster together. When we have strong leadership, collaboration, communication, and trust, and when we listen to connect with one another instead of listening to reply, we clear the way for better tomorrows. As a result, lives are changed.

⚙ MY ACCIDENT TRANSFORMED MY UNDERSTAND-ing of what a team is. I realized that it's not just the group of buddies you ride with, and it's not just the people you work with, but it's your whole network — all the people who support you and whom you support. I would never have healed my body, mind, and spirit if it weren't for my entire community, my entire peloton.

In sharing what I've learned, my intention is to help people apply these lessons. I see now that the values that made my emotional and physical recovery possible are the same values that can be applied to anything in which we wish to excel: business, athleticism, marriage, or any other part of life.

I wrote this book, first and foremost, for my daughters, Elle and Grady, because they were so young when my accident happened. Though mine has been a long, sometimes winding, and indirect path, I hope they can learn from my journey. While no book can contain or express everything, there are ways of being that I've learned along the way that helped me move beyond my last bad day. It's my hope that they resonate, at least in part, with everyone who reads this book and help you win at work and, more importantly, in life.

1. Be Mindful: Today it is easier to look at our phones than each other. It's even more difficult to look at yourself. Be aware. Be reflective.

Know your *why;* it makes your *how* easier. Know your values; they serve as your compass. Know your triggers; knowing them helps you quiet your emotional brain.

As Carl Jung wrote, "Until you make the unconscious conscious, it will direct your life and you will call it fate."

2. Be Accepting: Acceptance helps you to own what is. It sets up the possibility of letting things go so you can move forward. After all, fretting about the past will not change the outcome. Bad things will always happen to good people. These are life's way of making good people great. It gives them the chance to show that life is defined by how you respond to it. Acceptance is a powerful tailwind that pushes you forward.

3. Be Forgiving: When challenges happen or people cross you, it's reasonable to feel the emotions of anger, frustration, and worry — that's human. But holding on to those emotions doesn't serve you well. As quickly as you can, shift to a new mindset.

In 2012, my family and I toured the Auschwitz II–Birkenau concentration camp with Holocaust survivor Eva Kor. She told us that she forgave the Nazis. Her reason was not because *they* deserved forgiveness, but because *she* deserved it.

It was only then, when I heard her answer, that I completely released my emotions toward the driver of that SUV.

4. Be Balanced: The idea that life will reach some homeostasis with a perfect work–life balance is a myth. Maintaining all aspects of your life in harmony is more like trying to balance on a health club's BOSU ball. It can be done, but you must engage your core, keep a keen focus, and make wise choices. The moment that you forget any of these, you will fall off. It's easy to be governed by the fear of missing out (FOMO) and the pursuit of shiny objects. This makes balance difficult. Those who achieve their best know what truly matters to their happiness. They prioritize to help them gain balance.

5. Be Working: Hustle beats talent when talent doesn't hustle. There will always be situations where you won't be the smartest or fittest in the room. This is a good thing. Competition helps you level up. But know that a win is still possible. You always have a say when it comes to your work ethic, which will directly influence your success even when you may be outmatched. It's okay if you are not the smartest person in the room, but never be the one who gets outhustled on the things that truly matter.

6. Be Quiet: Life today is busy. As a result, it's easy to be consistently hurried. But as coach John Wooden once advised, "Be quick, but don't hurry."

If you want to go faster, slow down and find your quiet. Find moments to just be with you. You can call it meditation, centering, or just simple breathing. Just don't call it woo-woo. It's not. It's the secret sauce that will enhance your awareness, acceptance, and balance.

7. Be Kind: Kindness is taught by every major religion. When you are kind, it begets more kindness. Start by being kind to yourself. Be mindful of what your inner critic tells you. Kindness to others brings empathy, which is envisioning yourself in the shoes of others. It reduces stress, promotes loyalty, and just plain feels good as it ripples across your community (both local and global). Even Plato agreed with this universal sentiment: "Be kind, for everyone you meet is fighting a hard battle."

8. Be Giving: Give, but expect nothing in return. Just give. That's true giving. Many people just give to get. There's a big difference. When we give more and expect nothing in return, something wonderful happens. We actually receive more. Funny how the universe works. Listen to it more than you listen to your ego.

9. Be Vulnerable: It can be scary to ask for help. It's an act of vulnerability. It opens you up to judgment. This isn't easy. No one loves feeling judged, and we usually avoid situations where we might be.

But asking for help isn't a sign of weakness. Rather, it allows others to get closer to you — and for you to get closer to others. Accepting help builds your peloton.

10. Be Present: Be here now. You will never be able to change the events of yesterday. Don't be worried about tomorrow; it's not here yet. Detach from outcome. Be focused on the moment. This is what makes creating better tomorrows possible.

11. Be Curious: Ask questions for which you don't know the answer. Ask more questions that start with why, what, and how. Create the space in your conversations that will give trust a chance to sprout. Don't forget to be curious with yourself, too. You never know what you can accomplish until you ask yourself.

12. Be Attentive: Listen in order to connect with others. Don't listen to reply. Pay attention to what and how things are being shared. Be present. Acknowledge and validate what you hear to build trust with others.

13. Be Open: Allow yourself to be influenced. Your world-view is unique. It's special to you, your life experiences, and your beliefs. But, sorry to say, it's not always going to be correct. Listen to the life experiences and beliefs of others. Be open to the possibility that your way may not be the best way. Fight your ego's addiction to being right.

14. Be Grateful: Be thankful, especially for the little things — like guava juice in the mornings. Celebrate the little things daily. They help attract even bigger things to be grateful for. Plus, it beats the alternative — being upset or playing the victim. That action doesn't attract anything but catabolic energy, the kind that breaks things down rather than building them up.

15. Be Courageous: Fear is normal. Don't buy into the "No Fear" hype. Denial is a powerful poison. If you are truly striving to be your best, you will have moments when your inner critic will weave a fearful narrative. Listen to it, accept it, then move forward in spite of your fears. That's called courage.

16. Be Selective: You are who you hang out with. You take on their energy, and they feed off of yours. Be wise about who's in your peloton. Build your peloton with a diversity of like-minded people. Remember, you always have a choice in your relationships. You can stay victim to them, leave them, accept them, change your perspective, or improve them. Choose with wisdom.

17. Be Flexible: There will be times when life seems binary. There will be other moments when life doesn't seem to provide any choices. These moments will be difficult, to say the least. We all have them. Know that even though your situation may seem bleak, there are always hidden options. Keep seeking.

18. Be Your Scars: If blissful balance is a myth, then the idea that we are perfect or flawless is a nightmare. We are all less than perfect. You will make mistakes. We all do. Don't hide them from view. Own them. They define you and can make your tomorrows better.

19. Be an Inspiring Storyteller: Stories are powerful. They make sense of the world and bring us closer together. They build our peloton, but they can also tear us down. Resist telling those kinds of stories and share stories that motivate and inspire us to new heights. Elle and Grady, I'm grateful that I will be able to hear, see, and feel your stories.

20. Be Happy: Resist the belief that happiness will come from completing big work and life events. Happiness will come, but that version of happiness is often fleeting. Instead, choose to be happy now. Do the things that happy people do, like expressing gratitude and pursuing your potential. This choice will lead you to more happiness and success.

❅ *OVER THE YEARS, MANY PEOPLE HAVE ASKED* me if I wish my last bad day had never happened. My answer? No. Because on July 11, 2001, I told myself life would be different.

It is because I changed my perspective that new possibilities for every aspect of my life opened up. I learned that nothing truly changes until we do, and that the opportunity for us to change exists — but to take it, we need perspective changes that direct our eyes to a new place. Because, ultimately, we go where our eyes go.

Thank you for reading my story. I hope it inspires you to pause and notice where your eyes are looking.

Have fun storming the castle.

ACKNOWLEDGMENTS

Shift could not have happened without the help of a strong peloton filled with friends and family, including the following.

My parents, Jim and Judy O'Brien, who shaped me as a young man and provided the foundation for my shift. I love you.

The wonderful medical professionals at the University of New Mexico Medical Center, Lifeguard Emergency Services, Hackensack University Medical Center, Kessler Institute for Rehabilitation, and The Hospital for Special Surgery. In particular, Dr. Richard Schenck, Dr. Mark Langsfeld, Dr. Thomas Wickiewicz, Laura Fucci, and countless nurses, nursing aids, physical therapists, emergency medical technicians, social workers, and physicians.

David Kolb, who sparked my passion for changing lives through professional coaching.

Friends including David Bloom and Colleen Cooper, Kathy Graff and Ben Pinczewski, Megan Nishikawara, Will Miller, Derek McGinity, Jani Hegarty, The Colgate Crew, the community of Tenafly, New Jersey, and countless others who pushed me, let me draft, and shared a water bottle and a little GU along the way.

Darren Heath for his friendship, business partnership, and contribution to *Shift*.

Dr. Andy Pruitt, who helped me pedal in circles once I got back on my bike.

Elizabeth D'Angelo for reigniting my belief during a kick-ass spinning/TRX class in Kona, Hawaii.

My IPEC peeps in my peloton for their energy.

And Sally Collings from Red Hill Publishing, who helped me bring *Shift* to my daughters and you.

⚙ MICHAEL O'BRIEN IS PRESIDENT AND FOUNDER of Peloton Coaching and Consulting. As a certified executive coach, he has advised, motivated, and inspired Fortune 500 executives, entrepreneurs, and other difference makers. Before starting Peloton Coaching and Consulting, he was a healthcare executive and received his marketing degree from James Madison University.

Just as Michael's Trek 760 was the first of his many racing bicycles, *Shift — Creating Better Tomorrows: Winning at Work and in Life* is his first book, with more to come.

Visit him and receive his SHIFT Tips at
www.michaelob.net
www.pelotoncc.net
Twitter: @roadieob